FINNEGAN
self portrait of a fighting man

FINNEGAN

self-portrait of a fighting man

Chris Finnegan
Written in collaboration with Walter Bartleman

MACDONALD AND JANE'S PUBLISHERS
LONDON

ISBN 0354 04023 5

Front cover photograph courtesy of Don Morley/All Sport
Back cover photograph courtesy of United Press International

Published by Macdonald & Jane's Publishers
Paulton House
8 Shepherdess Walk
London N1 7LW

Photoset in Photon Baskerville, printed and bound
in Great Britain by Redwood Burn Limited
Trowbridge & Esher

Contents

What the Press said about Chris Finnegan

Chris has a way of summing up situations with a wit which makes writers curl up with laughter – and envy. Of them all, I liked his suggestion for the Finnegan family motto – 'Win or lose, drink your booze'. Peter Moss *Daily Mail*

Chris Finnegan grew up as a good beer drinker, but when he went into the ring, he was always fit. Nothing interfered with his training. No-one was fitter. Ever. Michael Herd *Evening Standard*

Chris Finnegan, with his puckish sense of humour, made my life as a boxing writer that much more fun. His courage and ability were never in doubt, but he earned my complete admiration for his total honesty inside and outside the ring. Colin Hart *The Sun*

Chris Finnegan was a pro's pro, respected by fellow practitioners and we hard-bitten reporters. He never cheated. He fought for a living but lived to fight. He did it with both guts and guile. One of life's he-men characters, I'm glad he passed my way.
Reg Gutteridge *London Evening News*

Chris Finnegan has given me many sporting moments to treasure since I saw him win the 1968 Olympic Gold medal in Mexico. But the words that are etched in my memory were delivered before his very last fight, the unforgettable light-heavyweight title return against Johnny Frankham in October 1975: 'I would not get in the ring and take the customers' money without being 100 per cent fit. I would not climb in if the will to win had gone.'
Sydney Hulls *Daily Express*

CHAPTER ONE

Doodle-bugs and maggots

They say that my birth might have presented a few more problems if a doodle-bug hadn't been churning away overhead, with everyone nearly crapping themselves as they waited for the engine to cut out and the whole bleeding lot to come showering down. Our Cowley home wasn't far from the RAF station at Uxbridge, which must have been a prime target, and the midwife attending Mrs Bridget Finnegan suddenly had her hands full.

I'm told that I literally tumbled into this world feet first, which isn't supposed to be the best method, on June 5 1944. That happened to be D-Day minus one, so I was well in time for the big fight. In fact I dropped out in the right-foot-forward stance of the southpaw, just in time to get an earful of the all-clear siren.

The happy occasion was also notable as the time when I got my first whiff of Guinness, for my Dad, who was a special constable during the War, was downstairs in the kitchen with three of his mates, prematurely wetting the baby's head.

I was the first of my Mum's eight kids to be born in England, and that should remove any doubts people might have about where I was born. It wasn't Ireland. My father worked there for several years and met and married my mother there, and the three eldest – Terence, Patricia, and Tony – first saw the light of day on the Emerald Isle. Then I came along, on this side of the water, and I was followed by Michael, Kevin, Celia, and Paul. That made a nice balanced Anglo-Irish family, for my father Patrick was born in Liverpool, while my Mum is a native of Newry in Northern Ireland. This explains why I always wore a shamrock on one leg of my boxing trunks and the Union Jack on the other.

My Dad had numerous jobs, most of them in the building

game, but he was a Jack-of-all-trades, getting the wages to fill all the hungry mouths wherever the chance turned up. He always put his family first, and although the Finnegans have the reputation of being a pretty tough outfit, we were all very cut up when Dad died some six years ago.

He certainly excelled himself when he joined 'Old Bill's' ranks during the War, and the fact that he knew quite a few lawmen has not been a bad thing for the Finnegans on one or two occasions. We certainly became well-known citizens around the Uxbridge and Cowley areas over the years, but I like to think that we have sometimes been a credit to this part of the world, as well as being a sodding nuisance at times.

We all went to the same school – St Mary's Roman Catholic – but I was never much in love with education. I didn't like it when I started at the age of five, and liked it even less when I left at 15. But there are some happy memories of the place.

I remember that we all took lunch to school, but there were some kids who always had something a bit tastier and more substantial than we did, and I soon tumbled that a boy in my class, who brought a decent bit of grub, fancied himself as a banger. At this time Kevin was in the infants, and one day I told this cocky merchant that I would bet him one of his sandwiches against one of mine that he couldn't knock my little brother over with one free poke.

Kevin would stand there as this kid took a swipe at him, but while the tears often came to his eyes, he never once hit the floor. Kevin's share of the sandwich – and sometimes it was chocolate – was a quarter. This went on for some time, but eventually Kevin got a bit cute, and insisted on going fifty-fifty on the profits. This made the scheme less attractive for me, and it was finally killed off when the other bloke got fed up with providing our lunch.

It was soon after this that Terence – always the Godfather among us – decided to organise boxing tournaments in our back garden. All the neighbourhood kids were allowed in, with Terence's assurance that he would make men of us all. It wasn't long before there was a queue of angry parents at the door complaining that their sons were coming home with busted noses and black eyes.

Not that Terence didn't do the thing properly. He used to get us up in one of the bedrooms, wrap blankets around us for dressing gowns, and march us into the garden in style. There he would announce us as Joe Louis, Sugar Ray Robinson, Rocky Marciano, Willie Pep, or any other great fighter who came to mind. While a couple of the other kids were a bit game, they soon tired of being bloodied up, and there were always those knocks at the front door, so before long we were more or less left to fight amongst ourselves.

Poor old Mum. Already tired of neighbours' complaints, she now had to put up with her sons belting the shit out of each other. But in our eyes the fights assumed the importance of world championships. Terence was always there, supervising, and despite all of Mum's efforts, the fights continued. Her favourite dodge was hiding the gloves, often behind the boiler, but we always managed to find them, or get others, and we'd battle on, often for 20 rounds or more, with no water or attention between rounds.

One of my chief opponents was Michael – we call him 'Maggot' in the family – and he seemed to bring out the bully in me. I belted

11

him again and again, but he was always coming back for more, taking on a sort of delirious gameness after each knock-down. I used to plead with him to give it up, but he would keep coming back, so one day I decided that the best thing I could do was to put him out of his misery with one good punch.

That was the day that I discovered I was never going to be a big puncher, because although I kept knocking him down, he was only on the floor for a few seconds before coming back twice as strong.

Michael's nickname of 'Maggot' is really down to Terence. As the eldest brother he always had the ascendancy over the rest of us, except for the odd times when he was away from home – sometimes for as long as six months as a guest of Her Majesty. These absences were usually caused by stupid things, like belting police officers, which is something they don't seem to like very much, and although we used to get our own way a bit more while he was away, he was very strict with us when he came home, and always made sure that things got done in the house and garden.

One spring day he came home and noticed that the apple tree in our garden was full of blossom, and he expressed the opinion that we were going to have a fine crop that year.

'Now I want those apples to remain on the tree while they're small and still growing,' he told us. 'Wait until they're fully ripe, and then we'll all enjoy them. If I catch any of you sods picking them before they're ready, you'll get a right murder off me!'

He emphasised the word 'picking', and believe me, although he was always pleased to know that we were helping Mum, he would have nearly killed us if he thought we were disobeying him.

A few days later Terence and his mate were down the pub, where he was sure to get pissed, and Michael thought the time was right to have a go at the forbidden fruit, which was beginning to shape up well. Unfortunately, our look-out didn't spot Terence coming round the back way into the garden, and he caught Michael perched up the tree with a mouth full of apple.

'Get down here! I'm going to remind you what I said!' he shouted.

Knowing full well what was coming to him, Michael pleaded, 'Hold it, hold it! You said we weren't to *pick* the apples, and I promise you I haven't picked a single one!'

Terence wasn't put off by that. Michael could hardly speak, his mouth was so full of apple, and Terence demanded 'How can you be eating those apples without picking them? Get down here!'

Michael was beginning to look a bit panic-stricken by this time. Terence wasn't going to wait forever, and there was no escape route. The only thing Michael could do was keep talking, and persuade Terence that no apples had been picked. To prove this he pointed to the apple cores, which, incredibly, were still hanging from the branches. He had eaten the fruit without picking it!

Terence looked in disbelief. He was speechless for a few seconds, then blurted out, 'You bleeding little maggot!'

And that's how Michael, who completely escaped the belting that had been promised to him, earned the nickname by which he has been known to everyone ever since.

CHAPTER TWO
Terence and the RAF

It was about this time that Tony, the second eldest of our six brothers, began to show signs of becoming a very good footballer. We used to play with a tennis ball in the road outside our house, and called the game 'drain-'ole football' because it was the drain covers on each side of the street that served as goalposts.

Terence had other ideas. He thought all footballers were no-good ponces, and that it was only fighters who should command any respect. Whenever he came home – usually pissed – and found us playing football, he would grab Tony by the ear and drag him through to the garden.

'Now then, get those gloves on and fight Chris. I've had about enough of that ponce's game. Come on, Chris, tear his guts out! I know you're younger than him, but you can still show him up and make him see that he's wasting his time.'

'Younger than him' was right. Three years' difference is a lot when you're young, and so the fights rarely worked out as Terence planned. More often than not I finished up getting done, and it wasn't until we'd fought about ten bloody hard rounds, with almost non-stop punches being thrown, that Terence would call a halt. Of course, we knew nothing about gumshields and protectors, or even what a bit of vaseline around the face was all about. I was usually absolutely knackered and covered in bruises, but Terence would be well satisfied.

'Ladies and gentlemen!' he announced. 'Introducing to you the new world champion – Rocky Tony Finnegan, who has just knocked out Chrissole Finnegan!'

Now that *really* annoyed me. I wasn't going to let anybody take my championship away from me, and more often than not I'd tear across the garden, leap on Tony's back, and it would start all over again. Terence would be well pleased.

'That's what I like to see!' he would cry. 'Someone with a bit of courage and guts!'

Then he'd give me a right bollocking.

'That shows you must have had a lot left. Why the bleeding hell didn't you do that in the first place?'

I often found myself thinking that he had it in for me because I was a natural southpaw. Terence had no time for cack-handers, probably because he'd been stitched up by a couple in the days when he fought as a senior before being called up to do his National Service, and thereby hangs a tale.

When his call-up papers arrived, he managed to get into the RAF, and that pleased Mum for a start. She had something against the Army, although she never really explained what. Terence, of course, wasn't quite so happy about the arrangement. After a few months he was looking to be away, and whenever he came home on leave he did nothing but complain. According to him, he wasn't allowed to do a real job.

'There are little berks shouting and screaming at me,' he moaned, 'and I'm twice the man they are.'

Mum and Dad usually managed to persuade him to go back, but the day finally came when he couldn't take any more. His uniform went in the boiler, and he was away, over to Ireland, where he stayed for about four years. Tony and I went over to visit him once at Christmas, and found him running around doing jobs here and there and staying with an uncle of ours. We had plenty of relatives in Ireland, and he never had any trouble finding somewhere to stay.

He made one trip back to England during this time, when he was included in an Irish amateur boxing team under the name of McAleenan – our mother's maiden name. He came over, won his fight, and was back in Ireland again without anyone being any the wiser!

But after four years he was itching to come back to England, so he grew a beard and moustache. For the first few weeks nobody tumbled him, but he was soon up the Uxbridge High Street fighting again, and we all knew that sooner or later he would be nabbed. He told us afterwards that on one of these occasions he was just giving someone the treatment when he overheard an onlooker saying, 'Here, look at that geezer! He fights just like Terence Finnegan used to!'

It wasn't too long before the inevitable happened. There was a fight outside a pub one night, and the Bill suddenly appeared on the scene. They got Terence, and charged him under the name of McAleenan. The magistrate didn't take long over deciding to give him the maximum – a six month stretch.

'Take him down,' came the command from the bench.

'Go on,' said the gaoler. 'Down the stairs, turn right at the bottom, and remember – I'm right behind you.'

'You don't have to tell me where the cells are, mate,' replied Terence. 'I know them a fucking sight better than you do!'

It was during this stretch that Terence's real identity was established, and that meant a further six months to clear his account with the RAF. Then he was free to start all over again.

Uxbridge was full of American airmen in those days. They had plenty of money, plenty of booze, and had no trouble attracting all the local birds to the bloody great cars they used to fly about in. It was like watching flies round a bleeding jam jar. This didn't go down at all well with Terence and his followers, and he was never slow to tell the yanks what he thought of them. As a result he quite often came home in a terrible mess, with his eyes closed or his face covered in stitches.

I can remember telling myself, 'I'm never going to get myself in that state – at least I'll miss a few of the shots!' I suppose that Terence was always too drunk to think about the consequences.

Mind you, he was fit, and a bloody hard grafter. There weren't many blokes who would take him on, especially among the Teddy Boy set where Terence was a natural leader. I was still at school, and didn't take much interest in weights, but I suppose he would have been around the middleweight poundage.

The hard graft came on the building sites in the area, where Terence worked as a bricklayer's labourer. It's a job they call 'the monkey', and that's just what you look like – a bloody monkey, running up a ladder with a hod full of bricks, and then sliding all the way down again without touching a rung. It was a competitive job, but carried good money, just as it does today. I later got to know the job very well myself, and I know no better way to keep yourself in good condition and to always have a good few quid in your pocket with which to booze and buy nice clothes.

CHAPTER THREE

Bikes and boxing

It was Terence who later introduced me to organised boxing when he took me and Tony down to the Hayes club. Kevin also became a member of the club, but I was spending most of my time with Tony, who was still mad keen on soccer. Give him a ball and he would play on his own for hours and hours, and not surprisingly he thought he could make it in the big time.

The rest of us laughed at such ideas, but we were laughing on the other sides of our faces when he got a schoolboy trial with Burnley. Even then the club had a bit of a reputation for spotting good youngsters, and for a while it looked as if Tony really would make it. He was already well in at the Uxbridge amateur club, and was the happiest of fellers.

Unfortunately he suffered a cartilage injury quite early on, and that wrecked his chances of really making it in football. I feel certain he would have made it apart from that, for he could make a ball sit up and had a terrific shot in both feet. His enthusiasm spread to me for a while, and I took a liking to goalkeeping. They reckoned I wasn't a bad goalie, but boxing was always number one with me, and I can remember getting carried right away listening to fights on the radio.

Those fighters were gladiators in my eyes as they entered the ring to the sound of fanfares, with all eyes centred on them. I imagined myself jogging through the crowd with the spotlight fixed on me – an individual, and not just a member of a team. My boxing idol in those days was Sugar Ray Robinson, back in the days before Cassius Clay had been heard of. Sugar was for me the god of all, although I was only about seven when he came over and lost his world middleweight title to Randolph Turpin.

19

But in later years, like most people who understand boxing, I became fascinated with Cassius Clay, as he was then known. I'd been watching his progress long before he ever changed his name to Muhammad Ali. I was 14 when I saw him on the box winning the Olympic light-heavyweight title in Rome, and as we all gathered round, I remember saying, 'That's my baby – you'll do for me!'

It was my father who made me realise that the professional game was likely to be a far different kettle of fish from the amateur, for when we used to watch the amateur international tournaments on television, he was forever complaining about the style.

'Oh be Jesus!' he would shout, 'What's all this jab, jab, jab about? If I was there I'd give him a terrible clip with the left and put him down for good!'

Dear old Dad didn't understand the finer arts of boxing. He was always telling me to go straight out and give my opponent a 'good old whack on the chin', not realising that it wasn't always that easy. Still, he liked us to box, and encouraged us boys to go up to the gym, even if it was only to save Mum having to come out into the garden and break up our boxing exploits with the aid of a wet washing-up cloth or a broom handle.

Actually, Dad was a bit of a comedian without really knowing it, and we all thought the world of him. He used to have us in fits, and would wonder what he'd said to set us off, but we had to be a bit careful in case he thought we were taking the piss out of him. We were a happy family in general, though we had our ups and downs like the rest of them. We always had plenty to eat, for Dad worked hard and was always ready to do someone else a good turn. He was also quite handy about the house, and was particularly keen on gardening.

Maggot was shaping up as a useful-looking boxer. He was another southpaw, and had quite a few contests at schoolboy and junior level, but he never boxed as a senior. He would probably have made a good fighter, because he's a very determined sort of bloke, and tremendously strong, despite his wiry build. He could surprise you with his strength every day of the week.

I wasn't the only member of this close family of ours to do well for myself. My sister Patricia enjoyed a wonderful career in nursing, during which she served as a sister, and eventually matron at Hillingdon hospital. Later she married a consultant surgeon named George Balmer, and they now live in the Lake District near his place of work in Manchester, and have two lovely kids.

I suspect she moved north because she'd had about enough of her brothers! Terence was in and out of the nick, and this alone was enough to prove an embarrassment to her. The doctors on the staff at Hillingdon were very understanding, but when junior nurses came out with strokes like 'I see from the local newspaper that your brother's in trouble again – we had to stitch him up the other night' it got a bit much for her, and she had to get away from it.

So she went to a place where no-one knew the name of Finnegan, and got on with her work in peace. We still see her, of course, and she never failed to send a telegram when a fight came along. Now she lives in a whacking great mansion and we're all very proud of her.

My other sister, Celia, married a mechanic, and they're doing

21

quite well for themselves. Mechanics was a subject which interested me as a kid, and at one time I was making some pocket-money putting track bikes together in the back garden. I was forever going round the dumps picking up frames, wheels, pedals, and so on, or maybe I'd glance over somebody's garden fence and see an old frame lying there. I'd knock on the door and ask if I could buy it, and more often than not they'd be only too pleased to get rid of it for nothing.

I'd clean up all the bits and pieces, hang them on Mum's washing line, and paint and oil them, fix the gears for fast getaways, renew the ball-bearings, and then sell them. The garden shed was full of spare parts for the bikes, and I was making a nice few bob right up to the time I left school. As a matter of fact I was earning less money when I left school and went to my first job than I had been before! As well as the bikes I had two paper rounds – one in the morning and one in the evening – and another job round at the fish and chip shop, where I used to clean the spuds and help out generally. There was the added advantage of a good meal of fish and chips each night.

My evening paper round included the RAF station at Uxbridge. I saw a lot of men there who were obviously as fed up with life as Terence had been as an airman, and I soon realised that there might be a business opportunity there for me. I started tapping them for boots.

'What size do you take, son?' was the usual question.

'Get me nines,' I replied, for that was a good standard size.

'Nines won't fit you,' they said. 'You want sevens.'

So I had to tell them that they weren't for me, but for my

22

brother Terence, who was working the monkey on the building sites. Actually I had a ready market there for boots, as well as any old jackets I could lay my hands on.

Another little ruse I had going nicely for a while involved the change from the price of a newspaper. The papers that I handled were three ha'pence in those days, and more often than not I'd be handed two pennies or a threepenny bit. I'd put my hand in the jacket pocket that was empty, and tell them apologetically that I had no change, although I was usually weighed down with coppers on the other side! At first it worked quite well, but the trouble with a trick like that is that once you're tumbled, the word gets around, and then you stand no chance. The inevitable happened one day, and from then on most of my claims of having no change were met by charming remarks like 'Give us the change and piss off, you little bastard!' I didn't really mind. You make a crust wherever you can, and most of the blokes on that camp were decent types who didn't have very much themselves.

CHAPTER FOUR
The woodshed

At the age of twelve I went through an experience that in my opinion really steeled me for a career in boxing. The memory still floods back whenever I'm depressed or have had a good drink. Even after all these years, I still get angry when I think about it, and often, if I'm in a bad mood, Cheryl will know what I'm thinking and rib me about it.

My reply is always the same – 'You'd be no different if you'd taken the fucking hiding I got when I was a kid.'

It's something which has been burnt into my soul, and I've relived the terror time and time again.

Terence's mate Paddy Davies was getting ready to celebrate his 21st birthday. The night before, Terence came home well pissed, having dropped straight into the boozer after work, and when he saw me hanging around he demanded a favour.

'Here, I want some razor blades, shampoo, and Brylcreem. Go round to Mr Le Mare's barber shop and get them,' he ordered. I pleaded that the shop would be well closed by that time, but he would have none of that.

'No they ain't pissing well closed!' he shouted. 'Get round there and get them!'

I gave up. You couldn't argue with the drunken sod. I bowled round to the shop, and sure enough it was well closed. Back I went to Terence.

'I told you so,' I said smugly. 'They're shut.' I thought that would be the end of the matter, but not on your life.

'Then go round the back and knock them up, the lazy bastards! They've never done a fucking day's work in their lives! If you don't do as you're told, I'll give you a fucking good hiding!'

25

When I made it quite clear that I had no intention of knocking anybody up, he flew at me, and I got about four up the darby before I knew what had happened. I had to think of some way to escape, because he was still making threatening noises, so I made as if to go, and he settled down and got stuck into his supper. As I reached the door I turned and threw the money at him and ran up the passageway. Naturally he came flying after me, and as I reached the front door I noticed that Mum had just put the empty milk bottles out.

'Stay where you are, or you'll get these!' I shouted.

It didn't make any difference to Terence. He just kept on coming, so as he closed on me I grabbed the two bottles and threw them. They crashed against the chimney breast at the side of the house and showered glass all over him. He only had his underpants on, and was dancing around from one bare foot to another on the splinters, yelling, 'I'll kill you, you little bastard!'

I believed him, too, but I didn't give him the chance there and then. I was away. I went over to the canal and spent the next couple of hours tossing in stones, waiting until he'd gone out on the beer.

Mother had had plenty of similar experience with Terence, and we had a system worked out whereby she would leave the hall light on when it was all clear. If he was still in the house she would leave the light off, which meant 'Stay away – the mad drunk hasn't gone out yet.' Eventually I crept back and saw that the light was on. I went to bed with a warning from Mum that I'd better be up and out before Terence awoke in the morning. If he got me, there would be hell to pay. He would probably make me put the gloves on and then it would be out in the garden for about 15 rounds of him knocking the shit out of me. I was only 12, and he was the same age as Paddy Davies – 21.

So I got up very early the next morning and went off down the road to get some logs for the log shed which I had built in the back garden. I didn't know when I built it that one day I would nearly die in it.

That afternoon, a hot summer's day, I was back in the garden, playing with ants and a big bowl of water with a stick across the middle. Red ants were on one side, and black ants on the other and I would direct them across the stick towards one another. They would fight furiously when they met in the middle, although the red ants always won. I don't know what time it was, because I didn't have a watch in those days – I used to keep time by the opening hours of the pubs.

Then came the feeling. The feeling of being watched. The sixth sense that spells danger. I looked up and there was Terence with Paddy, looking down at me from the top of the garden. I didn't like the look very much, especially as they were both pissed out of their minds, and I started looking for an escape route. The garden gate was out, because that's where they were standing, so I jumped over into the next door neighbour's garden with Terence in full chase. It was like the fox and hounds as I ran panic-stricken over garden after garden.

Terence used to let out a wicked roar when he had a lot of drink in him, and he was letting me have the full treatment as he chased after me. I was getting into an awful state, grazing myself on the fences and the undergrowth as I ran almost blindly for some kind of sanctuary. I didn't find one. Instead I got tangled up in a hedge, and Terence was on top of me.

He dragged me all the way back to the log shed, which was made of corrugated tin. On that afternoon it was like a furnace. The logs that I'd collected that morning had not yet been stacked, and were scattered over the floor, making footholds difficult.

There was no way out, and I was shitting myself at the thought of what was coming to me. I wanted to die. Sure enough, I got the biggest hiding I have ever taken. He punched me until I dropped, kicked me when I was down, picked me up and threw me against the wall. I was up and down like a yo-yo. It was no good lying on the ground after that guy had hit you, pretending that you were too hurt to get up. He would just drag you up, push you against the wall, and keep punching.

I tried to fight back as best I could, simply to avoid getting even worse treatment, but it didn't do much good. I didn't even have the energy to pick up a log and throw it at him, which was probably just as well, for I might easily have been killed. I prayed to God for some mighty strength which might enable me to do a David and Goliath on him, but it was denied me.

He eventually finished, with a smug 'That'll teach you never to throw milk bottles at me again.'

I managed to crawl out of the shed on my hands and knees, and as he got to the top of the garden I shouted, 'When I'm older and bigger than you, I'm going to kill you!'

I didn't swear in those days, but I've never forgotten what I took and what I said afterwards, and he's never forgotten it either. Sometimes now, if we meet in the pub, he'll still talk about it. He's always surprised to hear me say that I really *did* intend to kill him, and I think that his surprise stems from the fact that deep down we know we love each other, and we're very close. But there's no doubt – I meant it when I said it.

I've never allowed that Paddy Davies character to forget it, either. Whenever I see him today, I make him suffer. I've often walked up to him in a pub and said, 'You, you berk, do you remember when you was 21, and I had to suffer? You never even raised a hand to try and stop him.'

He usually pleads that he couldn't have stopped Terence even if he'd wanted to, and he's probably right. Terence was a vicious sod. I can honestly say that I've never been hurt so much – both mentally and physically – as in the woodshed on that hot afternoon. The ring has never held anywhere near the sort of fear I experienced that day – I was convinced he would kill me. If someone tied a hand behind my back and sent me out to fight Bob Foster again, there's no way I could be hurt as much.

Mum never found out about it. I didn't want to worry her. My other brothers got me in and patched me up, and as far as Mum knew, I fell off the swings in the rec. Another good reason for not telling her was that I would probably have been on to another good pasting from Terence.

He certainly was a funny feller. Usually he was very generous, thinking nothing of giving any of his brothers or sisters a pound note when he was flush. It was a lot of money to us, and we all thought him terrific on those occasions, yet he was just as likely to come home a few hours later, after a session in the pub, and tear one of us up for the slightest thing.

Yet although my experience in the woodshed made my later experiences in the ring pale in comparison, I don't think it was Terence who turned me into a fighter. The Finnegans get their fighting instincts from Mum. My father was a fairly placid sort of bloke, with just the odd flash of a very tasty temper, but Mum used to get really wild at times, especially if she came home and found us boxing in the garden. When she waded in with a broom the fights soon broke up – you simply couldn't get out of the way.

Providing for us all must have been hard for Mum, but we never went hungry, and with a family so keen on sport, we must have been getting enough grub from somewhere. In fact, all the Finnegans were good runners – brothers and sisters – and we always did well in the numerous sports days that were held in the Cowley area.

All the other kids would turn up in their nice white vests, shorts, and plimsolls, but we would just roll up our jeans and run in bare feet. We were usually successful, wiping up all the prizes that were going, and thought nothing of taking part in a race at Iver or Cowley and then running four miles to Uxbridge for races there. And if one of us was beaten, they'd have to take a right ribbing!

There was a guy called Pat Rippingale, who owned four shops in the Cowley area, and used to sponsor sports day races, giving out cards to the winners, which they could exchange for toys in one of his shops. We all thought of him as a kind of millionaire, and I can remember gazing in the shop windows at the train sets, air rifles, and all the other things a boy longs for. One year Tony and I both had cards, so we went along to see Mr Rippingale and asked for a train set from the top shelf in his shop.

'Don't be silly, boys,' he replied, 'you can't have that sort of thing. What do you think you've won – the Olympics? You can have anything from the middle shelf down.'

He would never budge, and even if there were a few coppers left over from the cost of the prize, he wouldn't let us have the money – we had to take a lucky dip from the tea chest in the shop.

I still see Pat Rippingale from time to time, and never fail to enquire why I couldn't have a prize from the top shelf. One day, when I bumped into him in a local pub, he got a bit browned off with the incessant questioning.

'Give it a rest, Chris,' he pleaded. 'What are you going to have to drink?'

I insisted on buying him a drink.

'OK, I'll have a scotch,' he replied.

'No, no, Mr Rippingale' says I, 'you must have a treble – my prizes all come off the top shelf!'

Eventually he got so fed up with it that he invited me to send my two daughters down to his shop, where they could pick anything they wanted.

CHAPTER FIVE
My first title

By this time I was really getting interested in boxing down at the club, but I was always a skinny kid and couldn't easily put on weight. My first amateur contest had been at eight stone seven, against a guy called Power. I won, and even got my picture in the local newspaper. But was I bleeding well choked! Instead of putting C. Finnegan underneath the picture, they put T. Finnegan. I suppose the type compositors on the paper were so used to setting Terence's name – and not always in a sporting context – that they did it out of habit!

Later in life I understood the frustration that Kevin must have felt – always in my shadow as a professional fighter until he won a British title. I'm delighted that he eventually got the credit and publicity he so much deserved. We would dearly have loved to be the first pair of brothers to hold Lonsdale belts at the same time, but this sadly wasn't to be.

Dicky Gunn was my trainer at Hayes, and he was terrific – a sort of father figure who was tremendously understanding and seemed to get to know everything about his boys very quickly. I got on very well with him, and he was always careful in making matches – never really dropping you in at the deep end.

However, when the London Championships came around, there was no picking and choosing of opponents. My first go at a junior title came when I was 15, in 1960. I had no money for proper boxing gear in those days, so I had to wear plimsolls and shorts that were never meant for me. After getting through a couple of fights without too much bother, I came up against a geezer called Stone. I forget his first name, but I knew bloody well that his elder brother was a pro fighter called Dave Stone, and a pretty tough one at that. When I saw him in the opposite corner I was worried.

'Blimey, I can't fight him!' I pleaded.

'Why not?' was the short answer from Dick.

'Well, look at him. He's got real boxing boots on and all that – he's the business!'

'Don't worry about that, son,' said Dick. 'He might have all the equipment, but you've got it all where it counts – in your ticker, so get out there and do him!'

So out I went, and we had a right old punch-up that nearly brought the house down. I won on points, and what confidence it gave me! I got so much out of that fight, knowing that I'd beaten a bloke whose elder brother was a successful pro.

Yet funnily enough, it was almost four seasons before I got cracking again, and I like to think that it was that long lay-off which helped to develop my strength and stamina. Too many kids finish up being burnt out when they're still young because they have too many fights in the juniors. Not me. The only training I became interested in was in Guinness drinking! I used to look at that old Guinness advert – the one with the navvy carrying an iron girder on his head – and think 'That's me!'

When I left school, I didn't plan on going into the building game, because I was always tinkering about with machinery, and my first job was in an Uxbridge garage. They went in for push-bikes as well as cars, and this was something that I'd already had an interest in via my bike-building exploits at home.

But it wasn't long before I found myself in bother with another feller working there, and an argument led to a bit of a scuffle. He was two or three years older than me, and I didn't come out of it too well, but I promised him that I would get my own back, and the chance came sooner than I thought.

That same afternoon I noticed him going down into the repair pit to work underneath a car, so I grabbed a high-powered electric grease gun which was capable of sending a thin jet of grease flying for about 20 feet. You don't need much imagination to work out what I did with it. He was running around the pit like a rat in a trap as I covered him in the shit.

Of course, not all the grease hit the target, and some new cars nearby got coated as well. Before long the guv'nor of the works came running out to see what was going on.

'Chris!' he bawled, 'you've got a week's notice – you're fired! What do you think this is, a bleeding beer garden?'

'Week's notice?' I answered. 'Don't you fear, Bernie, I'm off now!' With that, I jumped on my bike and was away, and that was the end of my first job after only a few weeks. I never went back to that garage, not even to buy a car, and now I never will, because they've pulled the place down.

I went from there to the monkey on the building sites, and although I've often been described as a bricklayer, it was always my back-breaking job to hump the bricks up the ladder.

Of course, the pay is good – it's fucking well entitled to be – and I got the idea from Terence, who was always getting togged up in nice clothes and going out on the piss with plenty of money to spend. It's also a tremendous way to keep fit and, as I shall recall later, it stood me in good stead when the Olympics came round.

Mind you, there was one occasion on the building sites that

35

nearly finished me off. The site in question was at Harmondsworth, and there was one other bloke working the monkey there who'd spent many a good year at sea. He was much older than me, and you could tell from his face that he liked a drop of sherbert.

He must have got fed up with me bragging about how much drink I could take, and the great parties I was having at the weekends, so one day he grabbed hold of me. For a minute I thought he was going to put one on me.

'See here, son, you think you can drink, don't you? Well I'll show you. We'll go down to the pub when we've finished and have a drinking contest!'

As it happened it was the day before we knocked off for the Christmas holiday, and the guv'nor of the building job had said that we could go down the pub, where the drinks would be on him till three o'clock. This old drunk and I agreed to match each other drink for drink until one of us could take no more.

We started with bitter, but I could sink that much faster than him, so after a while he decided that we would change to brandy. Christ knows how many we sank, but in the end he couldn't take any more, and I was declared the winner. He just went outside, got on his bike, and started out for home, but he hadn't gone more than a few yards when off he came, arse over bollocks, and he was out wide to the world.

The trouble was that I wasn't much better, and my mates took me back to the building site and laid me down in one of the garages that were being built. It was a very hard winter, with frost holding up a lot of our work, and that day it got colder and colder. I didn't even have a shirt on, following the frolics in the pub.

When I woke up it was pitch dark, and I reckon it must have been about four in the morning. I stumbled round trying to get my bearings, but I was frozen stiff and kept falling over shovels and forks and all that sort of gear. Finally I collapsed again, and it wasn't until work restarted at eight o'clock that I heard a voice saying 'Come on, Chris, wake up!' Some bright spark even cracked, 'Bloody hell, Chris is early for once!'

They soon realised that I was in a pretty grim state, so they picked me up, lit a fire, and made some coffee. When I started to thaw out I managed to eat a corned beef sandwich and it wasn't long before I was running the bricks up and down the ladder again. I'm convinced that that bellyful of brandy kept me alive that night, so at least drink has done me one great favour!

Eventually I got back to fighting seriously, but it nearly didn't last long, because having won the 1965 North West London divisional title, I was the victim of a diabolical decision in the London Championships.

I was drawn to meet Russ Pritchett in the semi-finals. His brother Johnny was at that time the British professional middle-weight champion. I made a slow start, but by the end I had the guy going all over the ring as I blasted him from corner to corner. There was little doubt in the Royal Albert Hall that night that Christopher Finnegan was the winner, and I thought that the collecting of the judging slips and the announcement of the verdict was a mere formality.

Perhaps it was, but not for me.

I think it's a pity that the referee doesn't have any say in the judging of amateur boxing, for it was obvious that the one in charge of that fight thought I had won. When the MC studied the score papers he had a puzzled expression on his face, and hesitated before announcing – 'The winner is Pritchett!' The referee was also wondering, and sub-consciously lifted my hand! I started jumping about and displaying my obvious pleasure, thinking that the MC had made a cock-up, but the joy was short-lived. There was some nattering amongst the officials and we were recalled to the centre of the ring to, as I thought, rectify the mistake in the announcement.

'Pritchett, in the blue corner, is the winner.'

Then all bloody hell was let loose. My own mob can carry on a bit, but on this occasion the entire crowd gave the decision the treatment, and it's worth remembering that most of those who go to watch amateur boxing know what a decision like that can do to a kid.

I really was very upset, and just couldn't understand it. Neither could the Press, who all thought I'd pissed it. It was just as well that I had no money at that time, and my wife Cheryl had to go up in the gods! There have been times since then when I've wished she was up there again, for she's had a go at quite a few around the ringside over the years, and her voice is of the strength that leaves no-one in any doubt about what she's saying. She can 'lord mayor' like the best of them when she's put out, and if she could have got her hands on one or two of those officials that night, we might have been in real trouble.

People have often asked me whether I found her vocal encouragement during a fight embarrassing or distracting. Far from it – she probably kept my mind on the job, because if I got a bit lazy or felt that it wasn't my night, she'd come up with a few remarks that left me in no doubt as to how I was travelling. If I did have a bad fight, I used to dread coming down the steps and meeting her at the bottom.

'You lazy git! You berk! What do you think you was doing up there?'

But there was worse to come in my life, both from Cheryl and the boxing referees. A couple of seasons after the Pritchett fiasco, Dicky Gunn thought I was ready for a crack at the ABA Championships, and this led to an incident that nearly finished my boxing career before it had really started. I began with the North West London divisionals on my own manor, and got through five fights successfully to win that title. I remember thinking how bloody hard it was, and how much harder it was going to get. It was a tough division, and among those I had to get out of the way were Johnny Frankham, who was later to figure so prominently in my professional career, and Ray Brittle, who also later won a professional area light-heavyweight title. Brittle was another man who I later fought as a pro, taking the Southern Area light-heavyweight title from him in nine rounds at the Anglo-American Sporting Club in February 1970.

But back in the ABA days we were fighting at middleweight, and there were quite a few useful blokes around at that poundage. In the London championships at the Albert Hall I beat a bloke called Mick Cain in the semis, and then won the final on points against a coloured geezer named Dunn from Chiswick.

It seemed that I never managed to get any byes that were going, and when we got to Wembley for the last two stages of the championships, John Turpin got a walkover, while I had to meet the midlander, Burns, in my semi-final. I've never had a really big punch, and had to go the full three rounds and take Burns on points, so when I met Turpin in the final I was knackered. But the old southpaw tricks stood me in good stead, and it was my fork that was lifted after the three rounds. Jesus, I was the ABA Champion, and no-one was going to be allowed to forget it!

What a berk I was to think such a thing. People forgot all right, and pretty quickly at that. I didn't get the trip I expected to the Commonwealth Games in Jamaica, where I had fondly imagined I would be soaking up the sun. They chose Turpin instead. No wonder that I referred to him afterwards as the bleeding highwayman! As it happened, Turpin didn't win a gold medal, although both light-middleweight Mark Rowe and light-heavyweight Roger Tighe – a cackhander like me – managed to pick up gold. I reckon I would have made it three golds for certain.

I don't think I've ever been so despondent, and I seriously considered packing the game up there and then. You start imagining that your face doesn't fit, or your background isn't right, or something like that. It's easy to convince yourself that you're not wanted in the England team with a name like Finnegan, and there are always those who remind you that your brother has been in trouble. Perhaps they thought I was some kind of hooligan or lunatic, and I naturally wondered what championships were for if they were not intended to find the best men for the job, irrespective of who they are and what their social background is like.

Even my brother Kevin thought I should pack it in, but Dicky Gunn managed to persuade me to give it another year. I met

Turpin again about six months later, and if he'd carried a couple of pistols he couldn't have done a better hold-up job. Henry Cooper was guest of honour at that show, and I can remember him throwing his programme down in disgust at the verdict.

Then Cheryl started on at me again to turn pro. Not that the immediate financial prospects were that good, but she reckoned that if I was going to get hurt, it might as well be worthwhile. Cheryl has always been a sort of unofficial manager, and although she's a noisy cow, Sam Burns has always been glad that she's been around when I've been under pressure.

CHAPTER SIX
Cheryl

It was funny how I first met the blonde bombshell. I was with a mate at a jazz club in Cowley one night when we spotted these two birds. I'd been out with one of them before, and she was a bit of all right. My mate, being a bit cute and crafty, dived straight at the one I wanted – Cheryl – and not wanting to start a punch-up in front of two young ladies, I thought I'd wait until his concentration lapsed, and he let go of her hand or something.

He must have known what I was thinking, because once he got a grip on her he never let go. Anyway, they were both staying at Cheryl's home in Iver, so we walked them home. We got near where they lived and started talking, giggling, and necking, but before we could get very far Cheryl's brother pulled up in his car. Her parents were worried that she was out so late, as she was only sixteen, a year younger than me. Her brother was quite a nice bloke, and gave us a lift home, but the trouble was that I didn't get the chance to talk to Cheryl, and soon forgot about her after that.

It wasn't until about a year later that I bumped into Cheryl again, this time at a dance in Hillingdon. I don't remember much about that evening, except that she kept treading on my feet, but at least we had a few dances, I took her home afterwards, and we arranged a date for the following evening.

Then she fucking well stood me up! You feel such a berk standing around on a street corner, and I was convinced that all the passers-by knew what had happened and were laughing up their sleeves. I promised myself that the next time I saw her, I would strangle her.

It was about a week later that I saw her on the street, and she gave me a load of bullshit about why she hadn't turned up. I found

to my slight surprise that my anger was fading, and being a glut-
ton for punishment, I asked her for another date, and she gave me
the old come on.

I arranged to meet her in Uxbridge, but I didn't know that she
was working there at that time. When the evening arrived, it was
pissing down with rain, and I had no car. As I sat at home wondering about it, I concluded that she wasn't going to come all the way
over from Iver in that bleeding awful weather, and I didn't fancy
standing under a bus shelter and getting my bloody mohair suit
ruined. In fact, we'd arranged to meet in a boozer, and as I didn't
realise that it was easy for her to go straight there from work, I decided to give her the elbow, and didn't turn up.

This time Cheryl did turn up, and met a couple of my mates in
the pub. When I didn't show, she asked them where I lived, but
they told her that they didn't think it would be a very good idea if
she came round for me. One of them told her that my mum kept a
lot of chickens, and that if she knocked on the door, it would probably be opened by a fucking chicken. She took the hint.

I suppose it was a case of third time lucky. I started going out
with another girl – quite a dish actually, who's had her picture in
the papers as a pin-up since then – and on one occasion a few
months after I stood Cheryl up I took this other bird to a dance in
Hillingdon. It was a place that Cheryl didn't visit very often, but
when the end of the evening came, I noticed that Cheryl was walking out alone. So I told this bird to wait, ran into the gents, out
through the window, and round to the front, where I got hold of
Cheryl and took her home.

Some of the blokes told me afterwards that this other bird was standing outside the khazi for nearly an hour! It wasn't until the bouncers came round locking up that she finally realised what had happened. But even then she insisted on going into the loo to have a look round – probably the first woman ever to get a guided tour of a gent's toilet!

By that time I was about three miles away down some Tube station giving Cheryl the treatment!

I started dating Cheryl, but the other bird was still interested, despite my behaviour at the dance hall, and I still managed to fit her in here and there. Until, that was, her sister came up to me one night, gave me a smack in the mouth, and started on me.

'Are you trying to make a monkey out of my sister?' she demanded. I replied that I didn't know what she was talking about.

'Oh yes you do, you bastard. You're two-timing her, that's what you're up to.'

I promised her that if I had been doing any two-timing, it would stop, and so it did – Cheryl and I became regular in our courting, and we've never finished and never will. We've had our rucks – big rucks at times – but we've always managed to sort our troubles out, and I guess that's how it always will be.

Mind you, the competition wasn't over. My mate Stan – the one who fancied her from way back – was still hanging around, although he had a bird of his own. The trouble was that he was a good dancer, unlike me, and Cheryl likes a bit of a dance, so one night, when my turn to buy the drinks arrived, he grabbed Cheryl and was off, even though his own bird was sitting there.

I got the drinks and came back to find Cheryl gone, so there I was standing holding his pint as well as mine while he had about

45

four dances on the trot. Eventually he decided to come back for a break and a drink.

'Here's your beer, Stan,' I said, and I poured the whole bloody lot over his head! He took it quite well – in fact Cheryl was more steamed up about it than Stan. He was more concerned about his new suit than the indignity of the occasion. Stan always had been fussy about clothes, though, and the story goes that on one occasion he was threatened by another geezer at a dance, and before he would fight he went into the gents and took his new suit off!

CHAPTER SEVEN
The Wedding

The question of naming the day was settled for Cheryl and me by circumstances. One night we were out with my elder brother Tony and his girlfriend, and while the girls were powdering their noses, Tony informed me that Pauline and he were getting married.

'Bit sudden, isn't it?' I enquired.

'Yeah, well she's four months gone,' he replied.

'Christ! Have you told mum yet?'

'Yes, and she's not exactly over the moon about it, I can tell you,' he said.

'Fuck it, that's put me in a bit of a position,' I groaned, 'Yours might be four months up the spout — mine's six months bloody gone!'

As luck would have it, Tony won a bottle of scotch in a raffle that evening, so we could at least drown our problems for a short while. Mind you, I still had to tell mum, and Tony had got in first. It was about then that my father had a big win on the horses, and that certainly proved to be a blessing.

A couple of nights later, I decided that the time had come to tell mum — there was no point in putting it off any longer. I waited around in the kitchen until everyone had gone to bed, and then made mum a cup of tea and sat down. She wasn't slow to see that I had something on my mind, but before I could say anything, she started giving me a lecture.

'I suppose you've heard about Tony. He's getting married in about three weeks' time, and it's a case of having to, which is a terrible shame.'

'Yeah, well. . . .'

'Now you've got a very nice girl, so for God's sake don't go and make the same mistake as your brother!' My mum's a good Catholic woman, and she was looking me straight in the eyes all the time.

'Yeah, but mum. . . .'

'You've got to watch what you do – you can easily get carried away.'

'Well, the point is. . . .'

'Now hear me out, son! It's no good getting married on the spur of the moment and under such conditions.'

Finally I had to shout, 'Mum, will you please listen? I've got to, I've got to! I'm in the same boat as Tony, and the only difference is that I'm even worse off! Cheryl's six months gone instead of Pauline's four!'

With that, mum made the sign of the Cross. 'Jesus, Mary, and Joseph,' she said. 'What kind of sons have I brought into this world?'

I said 'I don't know, mum, but there you are. Do you know if dad has any of that money left?'

Dad was delighted. When he came in from the night shift, I told him all about it and he roared, 'Oh be Jesus, this'll be great! We'll have two piss-ups! Make it a double affair, and we'll be pissed for a week!'

But it wasn't quite as easy as all that, because trouble was waiting round the corner as a result of what happened that night Tony won the bottle of Scotch.

After the pubs shut, we decided to go and have a curry. When we got to the restaurant Tony and Pauline went in first, followed by Cheryl, and as I was about to step in I spotted a couple of blokes coming along with their birds, and since I was a bit pissed I turned to them and said, 'You can't have a meal in here, fellers, the law's been down and barred us all!'

In fact there had been some trouble with fights in the area, and I thought I was being reasonably jovial, but these two characters obviously thought I was taking the piss, and suddenly I was flat on my back. The road was being dug up outside the restaurant at the time, and before I knew what had happened, these two had picked me up and slung me over into the fucking ditch. As I fell I bashed my head on a lump of concrete and laid there dazed for a couple of minutes.

When I collected my thoughts I found that my head was streaming with blood, and so I crawled out of the hole and asked Cheryl where these two had gone. She pointed to the restaurant, and in I went.

Tony jumped up when he saw me practically bleeding to death. 'Bloody hell, what happened to you?'

Some jack-the-lad down in the corner smashed one fist into the other palm and shouted, 'I done him! You can have the same if you like!'

That did it. I went diving straight at him through the tables, picking up soup plates, curry bowls, and even the pictures on the wall and throwing them at him. Almost at once it turned into a free-for-all, and we gave the pair of them a right beating, but the place was like a battlefield by the time we'd finished.

Then someone shouted 'The law's coming!' so I was out like a shot, nearly got run over crossing the road, and climbed up a telegraph pole onto a tin roof, where I lost consciousness again.

It must have been about four hours before I got my senses back, and by then it was daylight, so thinking that it was alright I climbed down and went home to bed. Nothing was heard for a couple of weeks, but on the night before I was due to get married, round came the Old Bill.

'Mrs Finnegan, we've got to see Christopher.'

I was just sitting down for my dinner, but they didn't wait for me to finish that, and within a few minutes I was locked up in a cell at the local nick. Later they asked me to make a statement about an affray in a restaurant in Uxbridge, and it was then I learnt that the geezer who had hit me first was insisting that I was prosecuted for assault!

I told the coppers that the bloke must have been mad, but they weren't interested, and made it quite plain that they thought bail was out of the question. Even my plea that I was due to get married in the morning fell on deaf ears, and I was left to sweat it out in the cell. The terrible thought came to me that I might end up doing six months, and I couldn't make up my mind which was worse – a six month stretch or the life sentence that was waiting for me round at the registry office!

So I decided not to press for bail, but Cheryl's father wasn't having any of that. As far as he was concerned, I might have been rigging the whole thing, and he wanted to get the villain who'd given his daughter one out of jail to make an honest woman of her. After a lot of argument and the production of some surety, he managed to get me out, and I went home, got spruced up, and went to the registry office. After the wedding, of course, we had a terrific booze-up.

Sometimes, when Cheryl and I are having an argument, and it's not going too well for her, she comes out with, 'Ah, but don't forget that my father bailed you out when you was in trouble.'

'I'm not surprised, when he knew that he was going to get rid of you in the morning!' is my usual reply.

But I don't want to give the impression that Cheryl and me are always arguing. We've had our fair share of trouble and strife, but she's a real sticker, and worth a good right hand to any bloke.

I remember one occasion when we were courting which illustrates this. We'd just come out of a boozer, which wasn't unusual, and had made our way to the bus stop. Cheryl then discovered that she'd run out of cigarettes, so being a young gentleman – I was about 18 at the time – I said that I would go and get some for her from the machine up the road.

I was just putting my money in when I heard some shouting going on – nasty remarks like 'Come on, get 'em off!' and 'Alright if we give you one?' As I came back I could see that Cheryl was the target for three RAF blokes.

'Go on, piss off!' I shouted. 'Get on your bikes before I come over and sort the three of you out!'

Actually I was shitting in my boots, but I felt I had to put up a show.

'Who do you think you are, Cassius Clay?' called back one of them. They were giving each other the nudge, and I could see that they'd made up their minds to do the business on me.

As they came across the street three-handed, I shouted, 'Now hold it fellers, for God's sake. Before we start I've got to tell you that I've got a weak heart, I'm blind in one eye, and I've got bronchitis.'

I realise now that the eye bit was one crack that took a long time to bounce back on me. Anyway, they hesitated when they heard this, and I decided to strike first. I chinned the nearest one, and he went straight down – I think he was the first bloke I ever dropped in my life! Without pausing, I booted the next one in the cobblers, and that left the big one.

I started struggling with him, but he was a bit big for me, and the longer I took to try and put him away, the more the other two were coming round. One of them actually managed to get to his feet, and things were looking a bit naughty, but Cheryl had other ideas.

The bus stop had one of those metal litter bins attached to it. They weigh quite a bit, but that didn't worry Cheryl – she pulled it off its hooks and as this guy was struggling to his feet, she smashed him right across the head with it. That was him out for the count!

Then a car pulled up, and someone shouted, 'Are you in trouble, Chris?' Luckily it was someone who knew me – in fact a bloke that I'd had a go at the week before.

'Looks like it, don't it? I've got three of the berks here,' I called back.

Addressing himself to the airmen, this bloke said, 'OK, he'll take you on one at a time up this side alley.'

I had an idea that he wanted to get me a pasting, but before I could say anything the biggest of the three – and he was a big geezer – said 'I'll go first.' So we walked up the alley.

'This'll do,' he said after a few yards.

'Let's go on a bit further,' I replied, 'I know the people who live in this house.'

Of course, I didn't.

As he turned to go a bit further, I belted him, jumped on top of him, and did the necessary, like banging his head on the pavement. He was soon finished.

I walked back on to the main road, shrugging my shoulders, and called, 'Right – who's next, then?' But seeing that their mate – the best fighter of the three – had obviously been done, the other two turned and ran.

'How did you do it?' enquired Cheryl.

'The old karate, love,' I said with a lot of swagger. 'It's easy when you know how.'

CHAPTER EIGHT

Target Mexico

I've never really cribbed about losing, or been one for thinking up all sorts of excuses. I've had bad fights in my time, and recognise the fact. My old woman has never been slow to remind me of it, either! But I learned át a very early age that the name Finnegan didn't exactly give you a head start in boxing, and there were always those looking to give me the elbow. I've already described my disappointment at not getting to the Commonwealth Games in Jamaica after winning the ABA middleweight title in 1966, but when I reached the final again in 1967 I was subjected to a dreadful decision.

The finals took place at Wembley, of course, and my opponent in the final was the Taffy, Alan Ball. I don't think anyone who saw that fight could accept the majority decision that went against me. What poxy judges. For my money they weren't fit to judge a cat show.

Ball was an experienced fighter. I think he'd had about 200 contests. But I outfoxed the bastard, and often had him slashing thin air as I moved out of his way with ease. The more I dosed him up with the old right jab, the madder he got and the more inaccurate his punches became. By the time the final bell went, I'd hit him so many times that even I didn't think there was any doubt about the verdict. But what a bombshell the MC dropped when he read out Ball's name, and the Welshman's fork was lifted. At first I thought another ricket had been made, but when I saw that this wasn't the case, I was really too choked and disgusted to say anything.

My supporters had no such trouble, and began to move toward the ring in a very threatening manner. The next moment everyone seemed to go berserk, and I feared for the safety of one or two officials – particularly those so-called judges. At first I kept trying to swallow my disappointment at losing my title in such a manner, but then my bitterness was overcome by the thought of what my mob might do, and the trouble they would get into.

A blond wig was tossed into the ring, along with a whole load of other junk, and the screaming and shouting increased. One official had a glass of beer thrown over him as he moved in to help clear the ringside – what a waste of wallop!

Dicky Gunn, my second and trainer, was heartbroken and pissed off out of it, but the trouble wasn't over by a long way – I don't think there was anyone in that hall who thought that Ball had earned the decision. The worst thing was that just before the next bout began, my younger brother Kevin climbed into the ring and squared up to the referee. They soon had him out of it, but not before millions of people had seen him on television.

Kev was suspended *sine die* for that episode. He had been doing well for himself at the Hayes club up to that time, and I reckon that if it hadn't been for my Olympic success later on, the sentence might have stuck.

A little later in the season, however, I was picked for the European Championships in Rome, which was one good point in the ABA's favour. I suppose there must have been a few officials in the hall that night who sympathised with me. The most important thing was that Kev was later reinstated, and we have since had many laughs over what we thought at the time to be a diabolical fucking liberty. But despite the disappointment with the Ball fight, I thought it might not be a bad idea to take the sport really seriously, with the prospect of Olympic selection in sight.

The ABA championships start with area contests all over the country, and in London the first step comes in the divisionals. I was in the North West London divisionals, and for some it can mean three or four contests in one day, so everyone's hoping for a bye while the others whack the bollocks off each other. I was always unlucky when it came to getting byes, even though in the early stages there are some youngsters taking part who shouldn't even be there. I think they're put in in the hope of providing one or two upsets, but to my way of thinking it's always been a dangerous practice. These championships are no place for a novice.

You can imagine my delight when turning up for the North West London divisionals to have my trainer Dicky Gunn tell me that I'd drawn a bye in the first series. And when my first bout came along, Dicky was bubbling over with excitement.

'Your luck is right in today, Chrissie boy, you've drawn Roy York. No-one's ever heard of him!'

Sure enough, he turned out to be very average. I was moving around, clipping him at will and thinking that I'd let it go the distance as a useful warm-up for the more difficult jobs ahead.

Then suddenly he came in, all arms and elbows, caught me over the eye, and I'm cut. Well, you know what they're like in amateur boxing – they see a drop of blood and that's it. It was only the second cut that I'd ever suffered, and they stopped the fight after just 80 seconds. I pleaded with the ref to be allowed to go on – I could have stopped the geezer inside another minute – but he would have nothing to do with it.

I've been cut a few times since then, but was I choked on that afternoon. As far as I could see, it was good-bye Mexico.

But at that time the secretary of the North West Division was Jack Forse, a cab driver who I believe later collapsed and died at an ABA Council meeting. He was a great bloke. As I sat breaking my heart in the dressing room, he approached Dickie.

'Tell Chris not to feel too bad, and not to pack up training. He's an experienced international and has done well for his country on seven or eight occasions. I'm going to put in a word for him.'

When Dickie told me this I felt a lot better, but I couldn't imagine them picking a bloke for the Olympics who had been beaten in the Divisionals, and somehow I thought that Dickie was only giving me the old gee-up. After all, if I couldn't get to the Commonwealth Games as ABA Champion, what chance did I stand of getting to the Olympics after losing this fight? And the ABA Championships went on and on, and I heard nothing.

Then heigh-ho, one night Dickie came round to my house and said, 'You're fighting Peter McCann, the ABA Champion! It's going to be a final trial for the Olympics, and will be held at RAF Stanmore.'

I was delighted, even more so when McCann had to withdraw through injury, and I ended up fighting a bloke named Barlow, who I outpointed. Johnny Stracey was on the same show, but I remember that I had not been training as I should, despite Jack Forse's encouragement, and I only just made it.

I know now that Jack fought tooth and nail to get me into the team, and I shall be eternally grateful. If I ever meet him upstairs, I shall thank him personally. I only hope I get there!

To tell the truth, I think I conned Barlow a bit. He was only 18, and knew that I was 24 with international experience, and he fell

58

for all my cack-handed shoving about. If he'd been in a different frame of mind, he probably would have beaten me!

After that, I started training like a bastard, not to forget the hard work I was doing in my hod-carrying job. When you're up and down that fucking ladder all day in the heat of the summer, keeping the piece-rate brickies going, you don't need to do any bleeding roadwork! That loaded hod weighs about three-quarters of a hundredweight, and there's very little let-up.

To give you an example of what the job was like, I was walking along one day on the site, and the foreman said, 'Where do you think you're off to?'

'I'm going for a pony and trap,' I replied.

'Come here,' he shouted. 'You're only allowed two shits a day on this firm – one when you get up in the morning, and one when you get home at night.'

I certainly wasn't frightened of the heat and altitude in Mexico after that!

Eventually I heard that I'd made the team, and I was to report for the first week-end training session. We were all pleased to learn that the thing was being organised properly for once, and that they were going to spend some money on us to get us ready. I became pally with Billy Wells, and we always shared a room when we were away with the team. I used to pull his leg that with his bald head, people would think he was my father.

This was also the first time, to my knowledge, that amateurs and pros got together, and it wasn't before time. After all, the Russians and all their mates are as good as pros, and the experience we were to get sparring with paid fighters would prove invaluable. Bunny Sterling was one fighter who was particularly helpful to me, and I like to think that I helped him as well, because soon afterwards he had two fights against southpaws, and licked the arse off both of them. I think Bunny's a great guy, and have always been sorry that he didn't get the financial rewards that his skill deserved.

David James was the national coach at this time. I'd never come across him before, and I wasn't too impressed by his methods at first. He'd cottoned on to some circuit training idea that he got from the Russians, and this was something I didn't go on. I'd done all my circuit training up and down that fucking ladder, and that was enough for me.

The first thing on the card every morning was a jog round the running track a couple of times to loosen up. Then they'd line us up for 100-yard sprints, and tell us to put everything into it. Obviously a bit of competition crept in, and we would really go at it for about four sprints. By that time some of the blokes – what I called the 'intelligent' ones – were thinking 'fuck this', but not yours truly. I was always full of pride and wanting to come first all the time, just like at the old sports days in Cowley.

When the sprinting had finished they would line us all up, and the first time they did this we thought the running was over, but no. They wanted us to run individual laps of the track with the clock on us, and we still hadn't had any breakfast. I was knackered, but there was no way out, and Terry Waller and I were the last to go, so at least we got a bit of a breather. This bloke Waller's built like a fucking greyhound, with a long pair of legs, and team

manager Len Mills – we called him Mrs Mills – was holding
Waller up as an example to the rest of us. That's all I needed, and I
decided to have a go and cook that berk Waller. Cook him I did,
and that wiped the smile off his face.

After turning in such a good time on the sprints, I was feeling
pretty pleased with myself, but tired, and when we'd had a
shower, I wasn't too keen on Johnny Stracey's idea of going to the
swimming pool. I felt more like a lie down, but decided to go
along, and we had a right lark about when really we should have
been relaxing and waiting for the next treat they had in store for
us.

It wasn't long before we found out what that was – down to the
gymnasium for the sort of work-out that none of us had ever done
before. It consisted of things like non-stop punching on the bag for
a full minute, whereas we had been used to jab-jab, boomp, jab in
our own time. Then there would be fast skipping for three minutes, and not the steady rhythm we'd been used to. It didn't do us
any harm, but coming so suddenly it was a bit naughty.

The worst was still to come, however, because when we got out
of bed the next morning, none of us could bleeding well move! We
were still expected to sprint, though, which isn't easy when your
muscles are all locked up. We'd all been using muscles that we
didn't usually use, and for a couple of days it was sheer murder.

I had come to the squad thinking that I wasn't really fit but that
I had eight weeks to work up to a peak, and here I was working like
a bleeding maniac right from the start.

Even so, I thought I could bluff my way along, but I started to
think differently when they moved in a squad of medical men with

a truck full of gear to measure this and that while we were training. They got hold of us one by one and stripped us, and applied
electrodes to various parts of the body, including the heart, and I
thought I stood no chance of passing. I could bluff my way round a
boxing ring, but you can't fool these fellers, and I was sure that
when they found out the condition I was in, they'd send me to a
fucking convalescent home instead of the Olympic Games!
They'd find out that I was a bleeding alcoholic for a start, and I
was dead worried.

When it came to my turn for a check-up, I was shitting myself,
and my fears must have shown because they told me to relax completely, to think of anything except what was happening.

You can imagine what I was thinking about.

After a while, the doctors started whispering amongst themselves, and I heard one of them say, 'I can't believe it.'

'This is it, Chrissie boy,' I thought, 'this is where you get your
bags packed and go!'

The oohs and aahs went on, and then the doctor working on me
decided that all his colleagues should stop what they were doing
and come and have a look at Finnegan. It seemed that they
couldn't believe the readings that were coming up, and after a
couple more minutes I got fed up, ripped off the electrodes, and
jumped up, declaring that I didn't want any revelation of my hor-
rible condition. I made it clear, though, that I'd still be willing to
fight anyone they put against me in Mexico.

They managed to persuade me to sit down again, and announced that they'd discovered that I'd got a very slow pulse rate.
So slow, in fact, that they could hardly believe the meter readings.

When I realised that I was a rarity, that pleased me no end!

One of their favourite exercises for monitoring pulse rate consisted of stepping up and down off a bench with a bag of sand fastened to your back. The amount of sand depended on your body weight. I thought this was a piece of piss after working the monkey, and so it proved, although some of my team-mates were falling about all over the shop and complaining of dizziness. Away I went, up down, up down, no bother. I was used to it, and as I carried on their bleeding eyeballs were nearly falling out.

When it was all over they got us all together in front of the doctors, who were due to tell us what sort of condition we were in. I was still scared.

They said that in general we were a very fit squad, but there was one boxer who really stood out as far as condition was concerned. His name was Finnegan. I couldn't believe it – how could I be so fit when I had been on the piss right up to the start of training, and we'd only been there for three days?

I nearly burst out laughing when they told Mrs Mills that I was the most dedicated athlete they'd ever known, and all the other blokes were sniggering, because they knew what I was like.

But it brought home a few truths to me. If I was in superb condition then, what was I going to be like eight weeks later? From that moment I determined to dedicate myself completely to being the fittest Briton ever to win a gold medal at the Olympics. Mind you, I nearly came unstuck during one of the training week-ends at Blackpool.

We trained all right, but most of the training was done on the birds on the holiday camp staff. What do you expect when you take a squad of fit young men to a holiday camp for the weekend? After all, I was only 24 then. Let's put it this way – if they'd included sex in the Olympics, the British boxing team would have won 10 gold medals, no bother.

One of the things we did was running on the sands, with all the birds watching, and that's how I came to pull a thigh muscle. I was in bloody agony, and some berk told me that the best way to cure it was to run it out. I reckon that was the worst bit of advice I've ever been given. The leg just got worse and worse, and eventually I went to see a physiotherapist on my own. He soon cleared the trouble up, but it just goes to show. If I hadn't done that, I would never have gone to Mexico.

CHAPTER NINE
A small matter of National Insurance

Before we set out for Mexico, I found myself in a bit of bother over national insurance stamps. I owed about £70 – you can imagine what it's like in the building game with all the tax fiddles, and my card hadn't been stamped very often!

So off to court I had to go, where I explained to the prosecuting geezer that I'd only been working three days a week, and hadn't been able to clear up the debt.

'When will you be able to clear the debt?' came the reply.

'Well, not for the next five weeks at least,' I replied. 'I'll be out of the country for all that time, and so I won't be required to pay for that period.'

'Where will you be, exactly?' asked the magistrate.

When I said that I'd be a member of the British team in Mexico, there was a roar of laughter in the court, whereupon the clerk – a slimy little bastard with goggles – jumped up.

'Oh, you're going to the Olympic Games, are you? As it happens, I was reading in the paper only this morning that the athletic team has not been chosen yet.' The smug little sod.

'Look, mate,' says I, 'I don't know what paper you read, but it couldn't have been referring to the boxers. I'm a fighter, and as I told you before, I'm going.'

He made it quite clear that he didn't believe a word I was saying. 'Have you anything that will prove this?' he enquired.

I thought I'd play the little bastard along for a bit.

'Well, I've got a letter at home confirming my selection – or at least I think I have.'

Back he came with 'Oh, Mr Finnegan, you're not quite sure, it would seem. I wonder whether you would care to return to this court in a week's time, and if you can produce this letter, then it may be that we will decide not to press for the five weeks you are away.'

So we left it at that. A week later I was back there, with the letter in my back pocket, but I decided I would have some fun with this smug little berk before handing it over.

'Well, Mr Finnegan, have you brought your letter? If so, we would like to see it.'

So I started the old tap-tap routine on my pockets, pretending to look for the letter without success. My face was getting longer every second, and I made out that in the rush to get to court I must have left the letter on the kitchen table.

'Oh how forgetful of you, Mr Finnegan. Now, can we hear the truth? You have no such letter, have you?'

'Hold on a minute, mate!' I shouted. 'I've just found it!' I produced the letter from my back pocket, and handed it to the bench. The magistrate sat there reading it, while the clerk is looking a right berk, and of course, the letter confirmed that I was going to the Games.

At the finish, the magistrate wished me the best of luck, and hoped that I would bring back a Gold medal.

'No problem,' I said. 'I'll bring you all my gold medal to look at, and what's more, there'll be no problem about the money that's owing.' With that, I shook hands with everybody, and set off for Mexico. Within two weeks of getting back I was summonsed again, but that story can wait.

Being a happy-go-lucky sort of bloke, I settled down pretty quickly in the Olympic Village. Billy Wells and I dived up the stairs a bit smartish and grabbed a room for two straight away, which was more than some blokes got. Most of the team were in a large dormitory, but Billy and I were older than the rest, and knew how to pull a stroke or two, so we were in before the others knew what had happened. For the first couple of days we didn't do any training – it was just a case of walking around and reccy-ing the joint.

Some of the countries had been there for about two or three weeks before us, and had hit the training hard, straight into it like fucking lunatics. I don't reckon it did them any good, and the one big credit mark I give to Mrs Mills and David James is that they decided to approach the question a bit more gently. It certainly paid off as far as I was concerned.

The altitude didn't seem to affect me, and everything was going smoothly as we moved into our training schedule. But it didn't last long, and we hadn't been there a week when I had my first brush with authority. There was a big communal recreation room where there was a discotheque every night and a bit of a general get-together between the various countries. But you could still feel the rivalry, and sometimes you could cut the tension with a knife. As I looked at them, with all the old powsie-wowsie going on, I got a bit fed up. The Russians particularly annoyed me with all their polite smiles and their bowing and scraping. I couldn't wait to get one in the ring and put one on his pissing chin!

Then there was all this badge-swapping lark going on, but I found little interest in this, or in trying, as some of our fellers did, to enlighten the foreigners in the art of playing darts. Some of them had even brought games out with them – ludo, snakes and ladders, monopoly, cards, and all that rubbish, and that Billy Wells was always sucking a tea pot, drinking tea by the gallon and always asking me if I wanted another cup. A proper mum and dad, he was.

The only game I play with cards is snap, and I only play that with blokes who stutter, so I usually ended up walking around the village – no more, I do assure you – and getting as many down me as I could. I had no weight problem, and would often treat myself to another steak in the cafeteria.

Most of the blokes would be back in the billet by half-ten, although there were no strict rules laid down, and so I was a bit taken aback when I bowled home one night at eleven and found the fucking door locked. I started banging on it, and after a few moments Mrs Mills opened the door.

'Get in my office!' was the only greeting I got from the miserable sod. I thought there might have been a message from Cheryl or something, but instead of that I got a right bollocking, and was told that I was a disgrace to my country. What did I mean by coming in at this time and letting down all those who had paid a lot of money to send me to the Olympics? I ought to have been ashamed of myself!

I couldn't take all that shit without coming back at him, and I said that I was confident that I had let nobody down. I also pointed out that everyone thought I was a no-hoper in the first place, and that as far as I could make out from the newspapers, I was only there to make the pissing team up. Anyway, when it came to ludo and snakes and ladders, that wasn't my cup of tea.

So Mrs Mills went off and raked out David James, the team

coach, gave me another bollocking in front of him, and asked Jamesie how I was shaping up in early morning training. David made it quite clear that he had no complaints on that score, and said that in fact I was one of the hardest workers in the British squad. But he did add that he could see the manager's point of view. After all, if people saw me out and about late at night, they might get the wrong impression.

I made up my mind that the next morning I would show Mrs Mills a thing or two. I was first out, and made sure that they didn't call me Arkle for nothing. I was lapping some of the other blokes round the running track, and really put on a good show, but I was still given official notice that I would be reported when I got back home for being a naughty boy and not joining in with the party games. I still wonder if that report ever went in. Somehow, I think not.

A couple of days later the Duke of Edinburgh turned up to tell us how Churchill won the war and all that old gee-up, but Mrs Mills has got an anxious eye on me. I didn't care that the Duke was going to visit us in our quarters – I was more concerned with the fact that I hadn't heard from Cheryl since I'd been out there. There was mail for everybody else – Johnny Cheshire, Micky Carter, Terry Waller, Billy Wells, Johnny Stracey, and Eric Blake – but fuck all for me. I couldn't make it out, and I was beginning to understand how our blokes must have felt in the prisoner-of-war camps waiting to hear from home.

I was wondering if the old woman had buggered off or pegged out or something, so in the end I sat down and wrote her a letter, telling her what I felt in no uncertain terms. I wouldn't like to repeat what I said, though I believe Cheryl still holds on to it. I'm not too good at spelling, and was asking Billy Wells to help me with certain words.

'Christ, you're not going to send that, are you?' he asked.

'You just watch me,' I replied. I addressed the letter to 'Miss Cheryl Mary Lucy' – that was her maiden name – and sent it to her mother's. I thought 'that'll fucking liven her up!'

Billy thought I was doing the wrong thing, and as it turned out he wasn't far wrong. The next day five bloody letters arrived at once – there'd been some mix-up with the mail – and as I sat down to read them I started to realise that I was right in the shit. She'd written to me every bleeding day! I would have given anything to have been able to pull my letter back, but it was too late for that. Old Billy was dead right.

Next thing I know there was a telegram for me. She was doing her bleeding nut. Then, while we were out training, she telephoned, and my dad was also trying to have a talk with me. They couldn't get hold of me during the morning, so she arranged to phone again at one o'clock, so I parked myself outside the office and waited for the call.

Then – just my bloody luck – the Duke walked straight into the office with Mrs Mills and all the other hangers-on, and just at that moment the phone rang. No-one seemed to want to answer it, so I dashed into the office. When I got in there I didn't know what to say. I know what I felt like saying – 'Excuse me, your Highness, would you mind getting out of the bleeding way? My old woman's on the blower, and it's a matter of life and death!'

But the Duke, bless him, sussed out the situation straight away, and when Mrs Mills confirmed that I was expecting an urgent call from home, they all pissed off.

On the other end of the phone, Cheryl was crying her eyes out, and I tried to explain it all. I think she eventually worked out what had happened, but she still promised me an almighty kick in the crutch when I got home! Then she started to calm down a bit, and I promised her that my next letter would be a passionate one.

With that nasty situation over, things started going better, and there was no more trouble with the mail. It's funny how letters from home buck you up, and you find that training comes that much easier and more enjoyable.

The next day the entire British team assembled in the main hall to listen to the Duke's pep talk. There were athletes, yachtsmen, sword-fighters, bow and arrow merchants, the lot – all sitting there in uniform. I never dreamed that Britain had sent so many, for you never seemed to see many of the bastards knocking about in the ordinary way.

After the preliminaries, the Duke got stuck in, and one of his main topics of conversation centred around the altitude question. Mexico City is about 7000 feet above sea level, and there'd been a lot of conjecture about how it would affect the sportsmen, but the Duke seemed to think that the whole thing had been exaggerated. After all, he reminded us, he'd played polo in Mexico City, and it had felt no different from Windsor Great Park. We should all try to forget the altitude, and all would be well.

When he'd finished, one of the officials asked if there were any questions. As you might expect, there were quite a few. As far as I was concerned they were all a lot of fucking nonsense, and mostly from the nice boys like the horse-riders and yachtsmen, who'd all been put at the front. Us punchy lot had all been bunged at the back where we couldn't embarrass anybody, but it didn't stop me asking a question.

I put my hand up, and Mrs Mills went a very funny colour. As far as he was concerned, the only things I knew anything about were beer and crumpet. Eventually I was noticed, and I stood up.

'I understand, your Highness, that the rare atmosphere didn't affect you in any way when you were playing polo here.'

He replied that I was absolutely correct.

'Did anyone think to ask the horses what they thought of it?' I asked.

That did it. The bloody place was in uproar, with everybody pissing themselves laughing, but from then on the proceedings became much more free and easy, which just goes to show what happens when a berk like me gets up and asks a silly question!

CHAPTER TEN
I'm a star!

When the draw for the boxing was made, I found that I was fighting a geezer called Titus Simba from Tanzania in the first series. I reckoned this was a good draw for me, because he was not one of the fancied runners, although one can always come unstuck against an unknown.

I soon found that he could wallop a bit when he had me down in the opening round, but I wasn't too worried and decided to keep the right jab going in what proved to be a good work-out and a contest in which I could get all the butterflies in my belly to settle down. When I did put the pressure on towards the end I discovered that the altitude was not the load of bollocks that the Duke of Edinburgh had made it out to be, and pacing was obviously the secret. I got the decision and felt quite chuffed with myself.

My second opponent was a kraut named Weold Wichert, who, like me, was a southpaw. He was a strong boy and had a good international record for West Germany. He gave me a really tough fight, and looking back I think he presented me with my hardest task, although it might not have been the closest. He really made me go, and hurt me several times, but in the end I got the majority decision. It was in the final round, when I went to work on him with both hands, that I did my best work.

My next fight was against the Yugoslav Mate Parlov, and here I secured at least a bronze medal. He was yet another cack-hander, and I began to understand those who took the view that southpaws should be drowned at birth. It was a bit of a rough affair, and we both put the nut in, but I didn't cut – that was the last thing I wanted – and although he caught me with a couple of hard shots in the last round I knew that I'd got him cooked. All five judges thought so, too.

Parlov went on to win two European titles, Olympic gold in 1972, and a world title – all at light-heavy, which was the weight I, too, graduated to later on. It shows that he couldn't have been a bad'un, although he was only 19 when we met in Mexico. In fact but for the diabolical luck which was to end my career, Parlov and I might have met for the European light-heavyweight title.

It would seem that he has become a really tough and dangerous fighter, but I reckon I could have completed a winning double over him. He doesn't like cagey bastards like me.

Now we were looking for silver, and luckily I had suffered no damage to my eyes as many thought I would. I was now the chief gold medal hope in the British team, because Waller went out with a busted leg, Cheshire got dumped on his arse, and Blake and Stracey were also out of it. Even the team officials were beginning to lap me up – old boozey bollocks, who most of them had been slating as a no-hoper only days before.

Some of the lads wanted to open a bottle of champagne after I beat Parlov, but Mrs Mills was afraid that it would send me off on the piss.

'Lay off, chaps,' he pleaded, 'we've still got a long way to go.' He was dead right

By this time I was beginning to realise that David James was doing a great coaching job. He knew the record of every bastard in Mexico, and had a room full of films showing them in various fights. He marked my card well about Parlov – that he was a rugged tearaway who liked to maul – but when I saw the geezer's nice flat nose I knew he could be hit. I was further encouraged when I heard that loud-mouth Terry Downes calling out from the audience.

'Put a drop of ketchup on your glove, Chris. He'll think it's a fucking hamburger and try and eat it!'

But the certainty of a bronze medal didn't really give me any satisfaction – after all, it's a rotten rusty colour – and I was hungry to get back into the ring. My semi-final opponent was a Yank named Al Jones, who was reckoned to be strong, smart, and experienced. But this didn't faze me, because with no chance of slipping off for a Guinness I was going around doing a bit of spying on my own account. Everyone thinks the Americans are shit hot, but I got a look at Jones, and he didn't look too clever to me.

He was a bit on the short side, and I thought that if I kept my right jab going into his moosh, he'd never get near enough to hit me. Mind you, you can't stop your arse going when the time for the fight draws near, and as we were driving down to the city, I was feeling more like having a good shit than a good fight.

We reached the British dressing room, and as the bandages went on I started feeling a bit better. After the bandages had been officially stamped, we went off to the gloving-up room, and that's where the Yanks started trying it on.

I was sitting opposite Jones, who was as black as the ace of spades, when who should sidle in and plonk himself down right beside me but George Foreman. They were obviously trying to psych me out, for although I wasn't going anywhere near that bloody great gorilla in the ring, his presence was a touch of the old evil eye for me.

I didn't let it bother me. By the time we went dancing down the aisle towards the ring I was feeling good, especially with old Downsey making enough noise for a thousand supporters! In fact Terry was very good to me out there, and gave me an awful lot of encouragement and advice which I'll never forget. It pleases me to put my appreciation on record.

Jones came out of his corner bobbing and weaving, and what do you know – he's another southpaw. Three of them on the fucking trot! This, together with the fact that the referee was the Japanese twerp who made a big ricket in counting out Micky Carter, who I thought was a good medal prospect, took me out of my stride for a second or two, and over came this shot which caught me right on the chops.

It didn't really hurt me – I have a habit of riding a punch – a habit which my trainer Freddie Hill has coated me about many times – so I went back on the ropes with my gloves tucked up ready to come bouncing back. Then this berk of a referee pulled Jones off and started giving me a standing bloody count! I waved my gloves at him in protest, but it was no good – he went right up to eight.

Was I bleeding mad! But it wasn't all bad, because the Yank was conned into thinking that I was ready to be taken. The smile was soon on the other side of his face as I whipped in a few jabs – bang, bang, bang – and finished the round in style. But that stupid referee had upset me a bit, and my corner had to cool me down.

David James reminded me that steady boxing was the way to deal with an opponent who had twice been decked and hurt quite a bit by the Bulgarian Simone Geogiev in their quarter-final.

In the next round I cut Jones under the eye, and it was my jabbing and moving that enabled me to escape his cuffing punches while I was gathering points with my counter-punches. Then the bastard hurt me with a left hook to the chin in the third round, and in came the Nip for another standing count.

Despite this I had no doubt that I had won, and the judges agreed by a margin of four to one. The poxy Mexicans didn't like the verdict and howled quite a bit, but I thought 'Fuck them – I'm in the final and in sight of gold!'

Mind you, I didn't feel so happy when I heard that the Russian, Alexei Kiselyev – light-heavyweight silver medallist at Tokyo four years earlier – had taken only 90 seconds to beat the Mexican Agustin Zaragoza in their semi-final. But I knew, suddenly, that I wasn't interested in the silver medal. I wanted gold. I always was a greedy git, and I made my intentions very plain.

Out in the corridor was the rostrum which they would produce for the medal ceremonies, and every time I walked along the corridor I jumped up onto the number one position. This gave my team-mates a giggle, but the more I performed this pantomime the more I got a funny feeling running up and down my legs, and I found myself wondering what it would be like if this really did come true.

It dawned on me that the Russian wouldn't be too popular with the natives after what he did to their man in the semis, and that most of them would be on my side, despite their reaction to my defeat of Jones. It's funny how so many people like to see the Reds licked, including some of their mates behind the iron curtain. I don't mind admitting that I said a few prayers before the final, and I like to think that the man upstairs is on the side of the believers.

Foremost in my mind was that all the people back home would be watching me on television and urging me on to win, and I became determined not to let them down. I'd already had letters from Cheryl telling me that I was boxing well, and all I had to do was keep it up in order to bring back the gold. And Cheryl is no bullshitter. If I box badly, she's the first to come in with a slagging.

My thoughts were also with my Hayes club-mates, who had chipped in with a few quid to help Cheryl while I was away. She was doing a bit of work as a typist at the time, but apart from that we had fuck all, and the money the lads handed over was a Godsend. So there were lots of reasons why I wanted to win, apart from the normal ones. It would certainly make things a lot easier for Cheryl and our daughter Pearl, who was five at the time.

I had watched Kiselyev a couple of times, and it didn't take me long to realise that he was a good puncher. But I also noticed that he seemed to tire towards the end of a contest, and I decided that my best policy would be to keep away from him in the opening round. Even so, I would have to try and do well in the first round, because a lot of these judges make up their minds early on.

October 26 arrived. The final. I think I was probably a bit too negative at first, and he got within range with a few shots, but without ever coming near to hurting me. My confidence came surging back in the second, and I got a bit more involved trading punches with the guy. In fact whenever I got inside I could hear him panting as I hooked him up the body. That was the music I wanted to hear, and I really started to believe that I could take this big Rusky. If I needed any confirmation that I was taking over it came with the ringside encouragement of the Yanks, including the late Yancey Durham, who later took Joe Frazier to the world heavyweight title.

'Come on, Finnegan! Let's go, baby!' they were shouting, and what with that and Terry Downes mouthing off like no-body's business, I was beginning to feel good.

There was no mistake. Towards the end of the second the Russian was beginning to tire, but my corner made it very clear that I had to put on even bigger pressure in the last round, and give it everything I'd got. This was what it had all been about. There were three minutes left, and I was determined to go like a bomb.

Out we came for the third, and I began to put it all together. I was fighting my bloody guts out, and with a minute left I suddenly wished we were starting all over again. I'm sure now that I would have knocked him out if it hadn't been for that careful start, but at least I could see gold at the end of this bloody rainbow.

The atmosphere was terrific, with everyone going crazy as we punched away, and with me, for a change, hoping the bell wouldn't go until I'd had a chance to put him away. But it sounded, all too soon, and as I strode back to my corner I looked Jamesie straight in the eye and said, 'Well, what do you think, David?'

James is never one to create false hopes, and while expressing the view that I had done more than enough, he reminded me of some of the strange decisions that had been made in these competitions before, particularly where a Russian was involved.

But as far as I was concerned, the gold medal was mine, and if the decision was to go against me, it would have been the biggest diabolical liberty ever taken in the amateur boxing ring.

Then we were called to the centre of the ring for the announcement. At first I couldn't cotton on to the jabber, but all of a sudden I heard the magic word which sounds the same in any language – FINNEGAN!

I honestly think that from that moment I switched right off – a state which lasted for at least two days. I shall never be able to properly describe my feelings as I climbed up on that rostrum for the medal presentation. The nearest I've felt to it was when walking down the aisle with my old woman after our wedding with me under some sort of spell. Only there was no gold medal at the end of that – only the golden rivet.

I can certainly remember standing on the rostrum thinking about my brothers – I knew they'd be drowning their bleeding selves in Guinness!

Then the Union Jack started creeping up the flagpole, and though I've never been in the Army, I don't think I've ever stood so straight in my life. I thought about the comedians who had been taking the piss out of the British boxing team with remarks like 'Tell us, how does your national anthem go?' and felt like sticking two fingers up at them.

They were bloody well hearing it now, and I felt so proud –

really great – proud of myself, Britain, Ireland, and of everyone who had had anything to do with putting me up there. There were even a few tears running down my cheek. That had never happened to me before, even when Terence half-killed me in the woodshed 12 years earlier.

Then all the lads stormed the ring, and carted me back to the dressing room in triumph. It wasn't until then that I found out what a close call it had been as far as the judging went. I'd got the nod on a 3–2 majority, with Mexico, Spain, and Cuba in my favour 59–58 and Thailand and India for the Russian by the same score. Bollocks to them. Lord Killanin, who also has a bit of Irish blood, I believe, had hung the gold medal round *my* neck, and I didn't give a fuck who disagreed.

I hadn't been back in the dressing room more than a couple of minutes, with all the whooping up going on, when a Mexican doctor came in and asked me for a urine sample, to check for dope. Now if there's one thing I've never been able to do, it's have a piss while someone's watching me. I can never stand at those long urinals you get in gents' bogs, with all the other blokes having a quick squint, and I knew bloody well that I was going to have trouble here.

Sure enough, I couldn't produce a drop. They were turning bloody taps on to encourage me, and some soppy cunt even started whistling, suggesting that that had been known to do the trick. Nothing. They started bringing me glasses of water, which I was swilling down, wishing it was Guinness. Still nothing. Someone suggested that I was completely dehydrated, but what really took me back a bit was when one of them suggested that I should put my tool under the cold water tap!

All this time the television people are waiting to take me over to the interview room. The satellite was passing over, and they didn't have much time. The delay was costing them a bloody fortune, and they were getting a bit agitated.

But the doctors were relentless. Unless I could have a piss, there was a chance that I would be stripped of the medal. That got me really worried, so I suggested that if they brought some beer instead of all the bloody water, we might get somewhere. I got three or four pints down me, but still no action, and the television bloke was jumping up and down like a bear with a sore arse. The Mexicans said that I could go for the interview, but an official would have to accompany me everywhere until I could produce the goods.

The interview was good fun, and they had Cheryl in the London studio saying her piece at the same time. People always seem to remember that interview, because when they wound it up by asking me what my plans were, I simply said 'To go home and increase the family!' I couldn't see Cheryl's face, but I think she was smiling!

With the interview over, I still couldn't raise a piss, and with a celebration meal laid on at a local restaurant, things were beginning to look a bit dodgy. But the two officials who were tagged onto me expressed their readiness to come to the piss-up – they probably saw that they were in for a free meal.

We'd been in the restaurant for almost two hours, and I finally realised that nothing would stop me having a piss now, so I jumped up and shouted, 'Who wants some piss?' The officials gratefully accompanied me to the bog, and I was pissing every-where – all over the place. They collected their sample and went off quite happy with our hospitality. The sample was, of course, negative, and it just goes to prove one thing – you can't take the piss out of me!

CHAPTER ELEVEN
Back home

A couple of days later we were heading for home, and as we came in to land at Heathrow Billy Wells, my constant companion, turned to me and said, 'Well, Chris, you're on your own now, it's all yours. You've got the treatment coming to you!'

I thought that he was winding me up, for although I was expecting Cheryl and my brothers and possibly my mum and dad to be there, I wasn't expecting anyone else.

As we went through customs, Billy gripped my hand, said 'Cheerio Chris' and the next moment I was engulfed and carted off to the VIP lounge. There were the mayors of Uxbridge and Slough – I live between the two boroughs – whacking out their official greeting and invitations for civic receptions. All the Press and television people were there on parade, my family and friends, some of them already half-pissed, and just like Billy said, I was getting the full treatment.

Eventually we set off on the short journey home to Iver, but I honestly can't remember whose car I was in or who I travelled with. Back in Cheryl's mother's house I began to come round, fortified by liberal doses of the black stuff, while outside in the street everywhere was decorated with flags and even all the moggies and dogs were running around with ribbons round their necks and 'Welcome home Chris' badges on their collars!

They really did give me the works, and naturally we had a good old drink-up, because I knew that the next day I would have to get down to business.

But I really had no idea of the extent that I would be in demand. The letters came pouring in – would I open this or attend that, how much would I want for a personal appearance? It was fantastic, and I found myself rushing all over the place, by car, train, and aeroplane.

Being a fucking nobody, I started to find it difficult to cope, and after a talk to one or two people it was suggested that the best thing to do was to get myself an agent. This I did, and the bloke I retained took a good look at things and told me that the main aim was to concentrate on getting the loot – and that would have to include my boxing. Cheryl was right behind him as far as that was concerned. She had been urging me to turn pro for a long time, but I was a bit more amenable to the idea now, because turning pro as the Olympic champion was a bit different from turning pro as ABA champion.

She told me straight. 'You've turned over the best amateurs in the world – now go out and give those professional bastards the business. From now on it's fighting for cash!'

Of course, she was dead right. No-one will ever really know the hardship we had gone through together, with summonses coming through the letter box for one thing and another – even one from the council threatening to evict us if we didn't tidy up the garden! When I pointed out that I was too busy training to worry about the garden, they suggested that I gave up boxing. What a load of berks – the same ones who were now lapping me up and almost pleading for my services after bringing back the gold.

My bleeding doorbell was nearly worn out by managers who wanted to get my signature on a professional contract, and they all made bloody good money offers. But I wasn't going to be rushed. We scouted round for a while, and eventually Dicky Gunn suggested that it might be worth having a word with Sam Burns.

He'd been in the game for many years, was highly respected, and hadn't done too badly for Terry Downes, whom he'd taken to the world middleweight title. So we set up a meet, but first there was the old question of the national insurance money.

When I went back to the court in Slough, I was no longer Chris Finnegan the hod carrier. I was a celebrity, with dozens of reporters, photographers, and newsreel men following me, and all the birds hanging out of the office windows giving me the big hello and cheering like merry hell. I arrived by taxi, and immediately got covered with streamers and confetti. Brushing myself off, I strode into the courtroom.

The little clerk put on a sickly smile – he had to really grit his teeth, the berk – and then came the congratulations from the bench. I invited them to have a look at my medal, and it was passed round the court. When all that was finished, the ferret-eyed clerk got his oar in by asking me when I would be paying off the insurance stamp arrears.

But there was a whispered consultation among the court officials, and it was announced that the outstanding amount of £70 had been paid off on my behalf by a certain Mr Harry Levene. This was, of course, the Wembley promoter for whom I later fought on a number of occasions, including my world title fight against Bob Foster, the big black sherriff from Albuquerque.

I was delighted with Uncle Harry, and with the slate wiped clean we all trooped out into the street where the mobbing, particularly by the birds, started all over again. And was I lapping it up!

When we got back to Iver there was another bunch of reporters and photographers waiting outside the house, and one of them told me that I'd got a lunch date with Lord Scarsdale. Apparently it had something to do with my insurance stamps. I didn't know who the bleeding hell Lord Scarsdale was, but of course he was a senior steward of the British Boxing Board of Control.

Cheryl and I had to get our skates on to make the date, and when we got there I found it was a right private toffee club – one of those gaffs where if you put your foot down a bit hard some old geezer puts his head round a big armchair and goes 'Sssh!' I wasn't used to all this, and I must say that I felt a bit out of my depth. I can't say the same for the old woman – she was more concerned with getting her hands on a gin and tonic.

But Lord Scarsdale and the lady he was with soon put us at our ease, and he turned out to be a real gent. We had a tremendous meal, and he asked me all about Mexico. I showed him my gold medal and told him all about it, and just as we're having coffee he whipped over a kite for seventy quid, and that nearly broke my heart. How could I accept it when Harry Levene had already coughed up?

I explained about Harry, and got a bit apologetic. I didn't want him thinking that I'd conned him for a nice lunch, but he wasn't bothered.

'Not at all, young man,' he said. 'But I'm certain that there must be other financial matters that need attending to – keep it for dealing with those.'

He wasn't far wrong. There were bills all over the place, and I was still borassic lint. I hadn't signed professional forms at this time, despite Cheryl's nagging, and the money was a real

Godsend.

But I was now more or less forced into turning pro, even though we had been getting up each morning to find the letter box stuffed with good wishes and all sorts of sums of money – nickers, fivers, and postal orders for a few bob from people in all walks of life, including quite a number of old age pensioners. They had all read about this feller who had been out of work bringing an Olympic gold medal back to Britain, and they wanted to show their appreciation.

It goes to show how people will rally round when their help is needed. They're the salt of the earth, and I would now like to place on record my most sincere thanks to all of them for their wonderful gesture. Mind you, how I could have done with that money before I went to Mexico. I left Cheryl to worry and suffer with all the financial anxieties, and this was never very far from my mind while I was away, even though being skint is nothing new to me. Cheryl and I have been in quite a few tight corners during our married life. Most of our stormy episodes have stemmed from money problems, and one incident stands out in my mind.

There was a particularly bad spell during one wicked winter when the frost and snow held up the building game for weeks on end. I was an amateur boxer, so there was no way that I could earn with my fists, except by flogging the odd trophy or two.

One week I managed to get in only one half day of work, and all I picked up was a fiver. When I woke up on the Saturday morning the fiver was in the back pocket of my jeans, and as I was getting dressed Cheryl asked me where her housekeeping was for the week.

I showed her the money – I wasn't in a very good mood – and told her that it was all I had. She wasn't pleased.

'Fat lot of good that'll be – it'll only just cover the rent! What about money for shopping?' she demanded.

I told her to give the rent man the elbow, and added that I would want a pound out of the fiver for myself. I had to have a pound with which to operate, to be able to go down the boozer. I know that sounds like a yarn, but you never know who you might bump into and find out where some work might be going. I reminded Cheryl that I couldn't go in there clean. I got little sympathy.

'You can piss off if you think you're going to get a pound for beer while I've got nothing to put on the table!'

The argument was just getting a bit naughty when there came a knock at the front door. I was getting into a violent mood, and when I opened the door there was a little man standing there in a black mac and a cheese-cutter, holding a big bag.

'What do you want, mate?' I enquired. I could see he didn't fancy the look of me, and after looking as if he was going to swallow his fucking adam's apple he said 'I'm the electric man. I've come to read and empty the meter.'

The rebate came into my mind straight away, and I asked him if there would be one.

'Yes,' came the answer, 'if you've got enough in it.'

I couldn't wait to get him up the stairs and get the meter opened. He started counting the money with Cheryl standing one side of him, and me the other. She kept reminding me that I was supposed to be going to the pub, but I wasn't going anywhere

BACK HOME

until this bloke had finished. After all, I wanted to see what sort of rebate we were going to get.

'Rebate?' she yelled. 'You'll get some bleeding rebate, I don't think. That's my rebate, and I'm going to have it.'

The poor little bastard counting the money was looking frightened to death. Cheryl was swearing at me, telling me that she'd put the money in the bloody meter, and I was swearing back, reminding her that I'd given her the money to put in the bloody thing in the first place.

Eventually I asked the bloke, who was putting money into little blue paper bags by this time, who the rebate did belong to.

'Well, mister, it usually goes to the woman of the house,' he piped up. That brought the smile to the old woman's face. But I wasn't giving up, and told him to forget this 'woman of the house' nonsense.

'Who' I asked 'is *legally* entitled to it?'

'Whose name is on the rent book?' he asked. I told him it was mine, and he agreed that in that case I was entitled. That was enough for me. I told him that unless he handed the rebate to me, I would report him. He was in a right state by this time, and his hands were shaking so much that it was all he could do to put the money in the bags.

There was still about twenty-five bob on the floor when he suddenly slammed his bag shut and ran for the door, calling over his shoulder, 'The rest is yours – sort it out amongst yourselves!'

Cheryl and I dived on the money like vultures, and started rolling about on the floor wrestling with each other and trying to pick up the shillings. I was even bunging them in my mouth to try and

91

keep them away from her, and Christ knows where she was putting hers. After a short while we started laughing at the stupidity of it all, and called a truce. Cheryl gave me half-a-quid, and I went off to the boozer quite happily.

CHAPTER TWELVE
Turning pro

The next thing was to meet Sam Burns. I'm not going to say how much he offered me, because it's none of your bleeding business, but I can say that I had been offered four times as much by two other managers, and I gave them the elbow. I chose Sam on his reputation, and it was a decision that paid off. We have enjoyed a wonderful partnership. I've never questioned any of his decisions or asked the sort of questions that some fighters are always on about, like what sort of opponent they're getting, and how much is in it for them.

I've earned more money with Sam over the years than I would have with some of those two-bob merchants who were knocking my door down with big-money signing-on fees. That signing-on fee would probably have been the biggest amount that I would ever have earned.

Actually I signed professional forms with Sam as my manager on television, with ITV's Dickie Davies as one of the witnesses. The stories started flying about that I was getting £1000 for my first pro fight, and whilst I'm not saying how much it really was, it was certainly the biggest purse ever paid to a beginner with the exception of Billy Walker.

And it was easily earned, for I stopped my first opponent, Mick Fleetham, in three rounds at the Anglo-American Sporting Club on December 9 1968. Of course, I now had Freddie Hill as my trainer – the biggest bully I've ever met so far as work is concerned – and without his help and advice over the years I would have been right in the shit once or twice. Freddie cusses and blinds all the time, and when I have started playing about a bit, he's threatened to throw me out of the gym. At the Craven Arms at Wandsworth, where he formed his Lavender Hill Mob, Fred's word has been law, and any who don't accept it can piss off.

It was the day after my fourth pro fight – a hard points win over Liam Dolan on February 11 1969 – that I had to go to Buckingham Palace to receive the MBE the Queen had awarded me in the New Year's Honours.

I was late getting there after dashing round to Moss Bros to get kitted out with a morning suit. In fact a pal had driven me as far as Park Royal Station, and we had done the rest of the journey by Tube. No cars for me in those days. I had cuts and bruises round both eyes, and must have looked a right sight. In fact the geezer on the door was in two minds as to whether to let me in, and we had to get the bit of paper out before he stepped aside.

So in we walked, the old woman and me, and I was shitting myself. But I needn't have worried. Everyone always says how charming the Queen is, and they're right. We were all well rehearsed, and when it was my turn to step forward she smiled and said, 'You look as if you had a rough time last night!' Then she went on to tell me that she had stayed up to watch me fight in the Olympic final, and that she had thoroughly enjoyed the contest. I felt great.

After getting the clobber back to Moss Bros, we went off for a celebration lunch, and I can promise you that those first three Guinness hardly touched the sides of my throat as they went down!

Meanwhile the personal appearance invitations were still pouring in. One that I particularly remember came from the Sportsman Club in Tottenham Court Road. They don't do a bad bit of grub there, and I've been back many times since, but this first occasion was in connection with the Miss World contest. They wanted me to float around with the birds, being photographed drinking champagne with them and generally browsing over them. It wouldn't have been too bad if I'd been on my Jack Jones, but I had to take the Duchess along with me, and she soon copped the situation.

I decided it was probably best if I stayed by the bar, and for once Cheryl agreed with me about that! The only warning I got was when one of the beauty queens got a bit close, and Cheryl hissed, 'Don't you bleeding well move!'

But to be truthful, I didn't see anything really outstanding. They were all pretty, but you've only got to walk around central London to see far more attractive birds, so the temptations weren't all that strong.

Shortly afterwards I was asked to take part in the Pete Murray radio show, and before we went on the air we discussed what I would be saying. Pete was really nice, and put me right at my ease.

'Providing you tell the truth,' he said, 'you can say what you like.'

We had a bit of a giggle, and I told him what I thought of the Miss World candidates. It seemed to go right, but I was never asked again, and I often wonder whether I cattled myself!

My second professional fight was at Shoreditch Town Hall. That was a lovely place for the real London fight fans, but they've closed it down since then, along with one or two other local halls, and I reckon it's a crying shame. On this particular night Sam Burns got a cheer and a few laughs when he came to the corner

wearing my Olympic medal. But that was the only sign of ama-
teurism in that famous old arena, and while I gained a fairly quick
win against Dick Griffiths, who I stopped in the fourth round, I
began to realise that the punters who follow the pro game are a
very demanding crowd. They aren't slow to show their dis-
satisfaction over the performance or the verdict, and as they're
paying, I guess they're entitled.

I lost my unbeaten record in my sixth fight. It was against a
black geezer named Danny Ashie, and I was stopped with a badly
cut eye in the second round at Shoreditch. I was really bloody sick
about it, especially when I learnt from the Board doctor, Adrian
Whiteson, that I would be out for at least two months. He put so
many stitches in the cut that he must have thought that he was
attending a needlework class!

Ashie made out that he did the damage with a punch, but no
punch could have inflicted that sort of injury – it was his woolly
coconut bonce that did it.

It was exactly three months before I had my next fight, and then
things began to go right for me again. I gained my best win so far
against the tough and very experienced Harry Scott from Bootle.
At that time he was the number one British middleweight title
contender, and a couple of years earlier he had outscored the leading world ranker Ruben 'Hurricane' Carter, who's now doing a
lifer on a murder rap. The fight was also significant because it
marked the moment when I moved up into the light-heavy brig-
ade, for it was made at 12 stone.

My first official fight as a cruiser came in January 1970 at the
Anglo-American Sporting Club, where I stopped the Spanish

Me, aged four – I always was a snappy dresser!

Top: Me (centre) with Celia, Kevin, Michael, and Paul.

Lower: Brother Terence, the one who did me over in the woodshed, pictured during a boxing exhibition in Uxbridge.

Me and Cheryl courting in Southend (top) and (lower) the wedding that nearly wasn't, with my parents on the left and Cheryl's folks on the right.

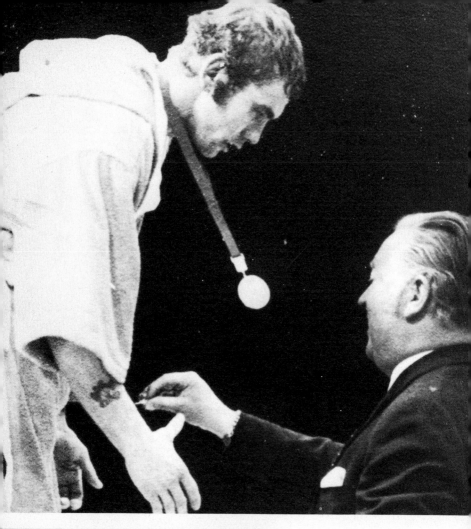

Above: Lord Killanin presents me with my gold medal at Mexico in 1968, and
Left: Sid James joins in the fun as I'm welcomed home from the Olympics.

Life as a pro. The top right picture shows action from my fight with Connie Velensek in Nottingham, when I won the European Championship. That was a happy night for the Finnegan clan, but the lower right picture shows the damage that 'pickle-head' later did to me, with Freddie Hill looking anxiously on.

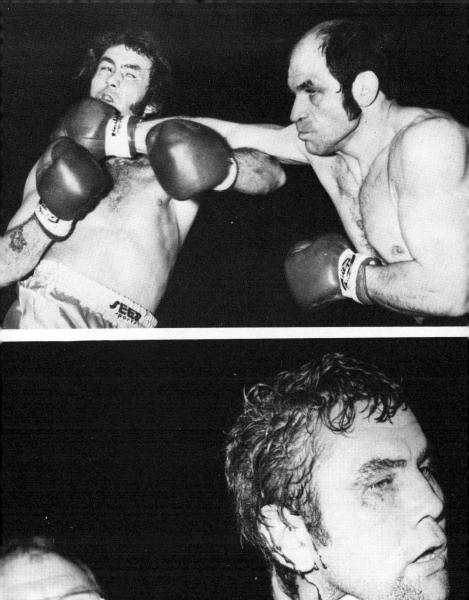
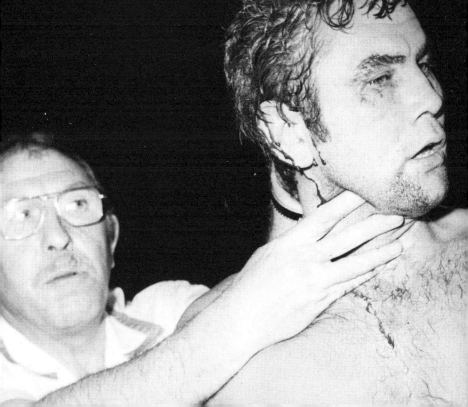

Top: The unholy trinity of Sam Burns (left), me, and that sadistic bastard Freddie Hill, without whom, as they say, none of this would have been possible.

Lower: The real champ of the family – my wife Cheryl – helping me to prop up the bar just after I'd lost my European title to Schmidtke.

Ain't she something? My eldest daughter Pearl, pictured in the garden of our home in Iver.

The proud father with his younger daughter, Ruby, pictured in 1973.

champion Fransisco Ferry in six rounds, and then I reckoned I was ready for Ray Brittle's Southern Area light-heavyweight title. The first time round Ray cried off with flu, but he declared himself fit and ready a month later.

I know Ray pretty well, for we come from the same area, and I had beaten him in the N.E. London Divisionals during our amateur days. As a professional he was unbeaten, but I completed the double over him halfway through the ninth round, and I had won my first pro title. I'm glad to say that Ray has done well since deciding to quit, and has a very nice little carpet business.

It was perhaps appropriate that the Area belt was sponsored by Courage – you can always depend on me to do well when there's a drop of beer about – and as I made my way home after that first title fight I had the impression that someone up there was definitely liking me, and that big things were around the corner.

CHAPTER THIRTEEN
The holiday that never was

Big things certainly were just around the corner, but not in the ring. I was running into a bit of bother with the old woman, and one of our fiercest encounters concerned a holiday we had arranged for ourselves in Torremelinos. We were slowly reaping the benefits of professional boxing, and she was really looking forward to it.

The night before we were due to go I went out with Kevin, and Cheryl warned me to be back early, because we had to catch a plane from Luton at about eight in the morning. That meant getting up at six, but as Cheryl had already done the packing, there didn't seem to be any big problem.

The problem came when Kevin and I got on the sherbert, and I didn't get home until about four in the morning. The next thing I knew it was six o'clock, and Cheryl was kicking me to get up, while I pleaded for another half an hour. I was shattered, still feeling half pissed, but she went on shouting and screaming and eventually declared that we couldn't possibly make it to Luton on time.

That was the challenge I needed, so I jumped out of bed, soaked my head in cold water, and slung my clothes on. But by this time Cheryl was too pissed off to bother, and declared that she wasn't going to go.

'Right!' I shouted 'You might not be going, but I fucking well am!' I grabbed my suitcase and made for the door. As I opened it, she calmly pointed out, 'You'll need this won't you?'

I looked round. She was holding my passport. I moved to take it from her, but she backed off and tore the bloody thing to shreds. I went fucking mad. I was scrabbling around on the floor like a fucking chicken picking up the bits, but at least by the time I'd gathered them all up, she had decided to try and get to the airport with me, so we all piled into the car and I drove off at a hell of a lick while she tried to stick the bits of my poor passport together.

Anyone who saw me driving that car towards Luton must have thought I was a bloody lunatic. We were taking roundabouts at 50, going through red lights with tyres screaming, and all the time Cheryl was trying to patch up the all-important document.

Luckily the roads were fairly clear, and as we got to within five miles of our target I was starting to breathe more easily. Then Cheryl dropped the bombshell.

'Hold it, I think you'd better pull up.' There was a lump missing from the passport – a vital lump as it happened, which left me with only half a face on the photo.

I reckon I must have lost about five pounds in weight with the sweat that had poured off me on that drive, and it had all been for nothing. I was up to my ears in temper, and without saying another word I spun the car round and headed for home. Cheryl was starting to look a little bit nervous, and asked me what I planned to do. I told her that I was taking her back to Iver, where I was going to kick her out of the car with her bloody suitcases, and then I was going off to the south coast for a fortnight on my own.

Unfortunately I then realised that she had all the cash in her handbag, and I was just pondering how to get my hands on it as we drove into Iver. Then a Dormobile drew up alongside us, and I recognised the driver as one of the blokes that I'd been with the night before. He said he thought we would have been airborne by now, and I got out of the car to tell him what had happened and what I intended to do next. The missus was ear-wigging as I got to the bit about going off on my own, and before I knew what had happened, she was screaming off down the road in our car, leaving me standing there.

I jumped into this bloke's Dormobile, and we tore off after her. We lost sight of the car, but my first thought was that she had gone home, so round there we went. No sign. The Dormobile driver couldn't spare any more time, so I decided that the best thing to do would be to go back to bed. She had probably gone to her mother, I thought.

I had just started to get some of the sleep I needed so badly when the phone started. It was her.

'Is that you, you drunken bum?' she shrieked.

'Right first time!' I replied arrogantly.

'Well, the boot's on the other foot now, ain't it?' she crowed. 'I've decided to pinch your idea and bugger off down to the coast.'

'Do that, and I'll strangle you!' I threatened, but she's a bit game when she's stirred up, and she was as good as her word.

When I realised that she had definitely gone, I tried to sort myself out a bit. She thought she was having the last laugh, but I wouldn't let her get away with it. I remembered that I'd been invited to a wedding that Saturday, so I cleaned myself up and started to think how good it would be to go to a wedding party and give it the full works without her being around.

And it started to look pretty good at the wedding. I was dancing around and getting warmed up, and before too long I was on a promise. Then the band decided they would take a breather for a few minutes, so a gang of us paid a visit to a boozer across the road. The only difference was that we had to pay for the wallop in there, but the bar was a bit quieter, and we didn't want to lose any drinking time.

Various people were asking me where Cheryl was, but I told them that I was finished with her – I didn't want to know. Then the boozer door opened.

Of course. Just my bleeding luck. Mind you, after I'd got over the shock, I realised that she had a frightened look on her face. Perhaps she thought I was going to belt her.

'Can I have a word with you, Chris?' she asked in a timid little voice.

'Can you bollocks!' I replied. 'Piss off! Go on, I don't ever want to see you again. I've finished. I've had enough. I want out.'

'But Chris, I've had an accident!' she pleaded.

She looked all right to me, so I asked her what it was all about. Apparently, she'd smashed the car up, but she and Pearl were all right, so I rushed outside to see the damage. She'd gone into something head on, and the bonnet was in a fucking awful state. It dawned on me slowly. You can replace a car, but you can't replace your trouble and strife and your kid.

I put my arm round her, and we went back to the party, where we had a great time and both got pissed as puddings. Another war was over, and we celebrated by going midnight swimming in a swimming pool that belonged to one of the guests.

CHAPTER FOURTEEN

Heartbreak
and a happy ending

After beating Brittle for the Southern Area light-heavyweight title, I went back to middleweight for a time, for I had no bother in making the poundage when I wanted to, and so I came to fight Tom Bogs for the European title in Copenhagen in August 1970.

Cheryl was a vital ally, because I had a few Guinness one night and the little plastic bag wouldn't stand it, so I no longer had a driving licence. This meant that Cheryl had to drive me to and from the Craven Arms gym every day, an all-round punt of about 300 miles a week.

The chance to fight Bogs came after his intended opponent, Mark Rowe, dropped out with an arm injury. Sam Burns got an offer for me to take his place, and although I'd only had 14 professional fights and wouldn't normally have come to the European title for another couple of years, we jumped at the chance.

I'd seen Bogs on television once. He'd taken on Les McAteer, the British champion, and destroyed him. He knocked shit out of McAteer for eleven rounds and then dropped him, so everywhere I went people were saying that Sam Burns would do well to keep me out of the way of that character. They did their best to put the fear of Christ into me.

I must admit that the situation wasn't very promising. McAteer wasn't the only British middleweight that Bogs had done. Although he rarely fought outside Denmark, he had an impressive record, which included victories against Harry Scott, Wally Swift, and John McCormack. But Sam Burns reckoned I could handle it.

When we got to Denmark we were made very welcome, and I took a liking to the country straight away, but at the weigh-in

Bogs made it clear that he thought I was only there to make up the numbers, and treated me like a bit of bleeding dirt. No respect at all.

He sodding well respected me by the time we'd finished.

The fight was in the open air at a football ground, and I took him the full 15 rounds in a right battle. There wasn't all that much in it at the end, and if it hadn't been for the scoring of the diabolical kraut referee, Herbert Tomser, I reckon I would have made it. Tomser scored four rounds for Bogs, *eleven* level, and fuck all for me.

Although I suffered a cut in the 13th, Bogsy had to be taken to the fucking hospital after I'd finished with him, and then he gave the elbow to offers of a return. I reckon he knew how lucky he was. At least I'd burst his bleeding bubble. And his nose.

So now Finnegan was in the big league. There was talk of me fighting Rowe for the British middleweight title, but that never came off, and my next fight, three months later, was against Eddie Avoth for the British and Commonwealth light-heavyweight titles.

I was put forward as a challenger by the Board of Control, and purse offers were invited. Jack Solomons got it with a bid of £3745, and said that he would stage the fight on Sunday, January 24 1971.

Now Sam Burns and Jack Solomons are not the best of buddies. I don't think one would give the other a drink of water if he was dying of thirst in the desert. That caused problems. Sam didn't want me to box on a Sunday at the World Sporting Club because the Anglo-American Sporting Club, further down Park Lane, had a European featherweight title fight the following night. But we could hardly say that in public, so the reasons put forward against a Sunday fight were that it was against my Roman Catholic principles to fight on the sabbath!

I pointed out to Sam that there was nothing in the Bible which precluded me fighting on a Sunday, but Sam isn't easily put off when he starts, and in his best Yiddisher style he told me that according to my religion I was ordered to rest. He pointed out that God had had a blow on a Sunday, and so must I.

I began to get the message. It would give the Press something to talk about, and so I put it to them that as I was a religious lad I couldn't agree to fight on a Sunday.

Sam patted me fondly on the head. 'That's a good boy. A good Christian boy!'

I played my part to the full, bringing out the rosary and all that old mularky, but then we found out that Avoth was also a Catholic, and he wasn't complaining. So in the end we had to swallow our pride, and with the promise of a European title fight for the winner we agreed to the Sunday date – the first in Britain since 1929.

A mate of mine had a Roller – a Rolls Royce – and he suggested that we turned up for the weigh-in in style, so when we arrived at Solomons' gym in Great Windmill Street there was a right mob outside to welcome us. I climbed the stairs to his pony gym fingering the rosary beads and muttering a few Hail Marys and contritions to make it look the real business. Solomons had a funny expression on his face. When we got to the scales, the nonsense had to stop, and then the photographers started clamouring round for the traditional 'shaking hands' pictures.

Avoth started it. 'Come on now, Chris boyo,' in his thick Welsh accent, 'I'm not going to bite you!'

'Too fucking right, you're not,' I replied. 'You're the one that's going to get chewed up. Tonight!'

We spent the rest of the day relaxing, and eventually the time came for us to set out for the Grosvenor House. All my tribe were there in their hired monkey suits, which is the form at the top dinner-boxing clubs, and my Dad was among them.

I thought I'd give him a thrill by introducing him to Sean Connery, but dear old Dad didn't know Connery from Adam, and said, 'Sure and I'm glad to meet you, Sean. Which part of Ireland did you come from to see my son fight?'

It was when we were on our way from the dressing room to the ring that Solomons had his own back on us for the religious caper. Instead of the usual fanfares, I was played into the ring to the strains of 'Never on a Sunday'.

So the rotten old bastard had had his little joke, and I started wishing that I'd gone through with my earlier idea of having four altar boys accompanying me to the ring, with a wired-up halo over my head! At least I was now determined to knock this boy out – and I did.

But I made him suffer first. I think he almost ate my right jab. It was like Chinese torture for him and Solomons, and when referee Roland Dakin stopped the fight with about a minute of the fifteenth round left, Avoth's face looked like a dug-up road. He'd had a little bit of the action in the early rounds, for I'm never a very fast starter, and I'd used the warming-up period to see if he could hurt me. Could he balls! My right eye cut in the seventh, but Freddie did a marvellous job on it, and it didn't really trouble me.

I mauled that Welshman. His gumshield was out five times. The papers described it as a massacre, and Avoth's manager, Eddie Thomas, was quoted as saying that the fight should have been stopped sooner.

At least I'd taught Solomons that it was a dangerous business to interfere with my usual Sunday night piss-up. Actually I could have got a postponement if I'd wanted one, because I pulled a back muscle and couldn't train for four days, but the Arsenal doctor, Alan Thomas, soon got his magic hands to work, and it was he who saved the fight.

The champagne flowed fast and furious back in the dressing room. My brothers were getting really stewed. After all, I'd now had only 16 pro fights, and I'd destroyed a bloke who had half a century of fights behind him.

Then the door opened, and in walked Conny Velensek, the European champion. He'd been dogging me out during the fight, and wasn't wearing the toupee he usually had for social occasions. We shook hands, and someone mentioned that I would be his next challenger. I turned to Freddie Hill.

'Gawd blimey, Fred, he looks a fucking sight older than you do!'

Freddie wasn't too happy about that remark, but his displeasure was masked by all the laughter, and after the Jerry had pissed off we got on with the celebrations. The European title fight was fixed for May 5 1971 in Berlin, and before that I had one warm-up bout. It didn't last long. I beat the American Pete Riccitelli in less than four rounds in Manchester.

When we got to Berlin, we refused all offers of German sparring partners. I don't trust the Krauts, and Freddie told them where they could go. Actually we had done all the hard work before we came away, but we had to put on a bit of a show for the promoter so that he could knock a few more tickets out, so it was roadwork every morning and the gym every evening.

I always thought I could take Velensek, right from the moment he came into my dressing room after the Avoth fight. He was made to measure for me. And after my usual quiet start I began knocking all kinds of shit out of him. The old right jab and left cross technique couldn't miss, and before long he had a bump on his head the size of a bleeding egg. It started to look as if he was growing another head.

At the end of the 13th he sat on his stool and started mumbling away, and Sam and Freddie started saying that he couldn't possibly come out for any more. I thought so, too. He looked done for. He was black and blue all over, cut and bruised, and looking right knackered. From what I could gather he didn't want to come out, but his manager slapped him on the arse as he stood up and pushed him out. I carried on battering him round the ring, but I couldn't put the little tank down.

I was almost breaking my hands on his bald head as he came in grabbing and holding. It was like trying to crush a cast-iron dwarf. He was still there when the final bell went, and as I went back to my corner my blokes, reinforced by the ever-present Mickey Duff, showered me with congratulations. They were sure I'd done it, but I'd been disappointed before, and I told them to wait until I'd got the decision.

Duff was more certain than anybody, but Velensek's mob had climbed into the ring and put a fucking great laurel wreath round his head. It was heavy, and with the striping he'd taken it was all he could do to hold his head up. Then they hoisted him shoulder high, and started running round the ring with him.

He did look well. He looked as if he'd been fighting ten tigers. Then the scorecards of the referee and two judges were collected, and they came up with a pissing draw!

I dragged myself back to the hotel, showered down, and was feeling so choked that I decided to go out for a drink. All the mob came with me, and we had a good piss-up, even by German standards! Everyone we met thought that I'd done enough to win, and not only because I was buying the beer.

One of the German papers said, 'The punishment Velensek had to take in the final rounds, when his left eye was virtually closed, was almost inhuman.'

Another said, 'It was a clear present for the defending Champion – an obvious discrimination against the Briton and a new scandal for already discredited professional boxing.'

The British Press were of the same mind. Good judges like George Whiting, Reg Gutteridge, and Peter Wilson all thought it was a diabolical verdict, and they were right. Velensek was stretchered from his dressing room to hospital with exhaustion and a face like a stamped-on melon.

But he was still champion, and when the talk of a return started, Sam Burns vowed that we wouldn't fight in Germany, where a local fighter had never lost a European title. At least the after-the-

109

fight piss-up was charged up to the promoter. I'd been stitched up, and now I was doing a little stitching-up on my own account!

There was another big welcome for us when we got back to Heathrow, because the fight had been televised almost live, and everyone knew that I'd been the victim of the fucking Krauts. It seemed that the villain of the piece had been the Spanish referee, Sanchez Vilar, who had been on the point of stopping the fight, and then gave it to Velensek 72–71. The Austrian judge gave it to me 62–59, and Luxembourg's Arsene Klopp made it a draw. Arsene? His name should have been arsehole!

Now everyone wanted to know when the return would be. We didn't have to wait long – about six months – and during that time I had three fights, beating Bob Benoit and Roger Rouse inside the distance, and getting a ten-round points decision over Hal Carroll.

The return was eventually fixed for February 1972 at Nottingham ice rink, and we were well prepared. We knew the geezer well, and felt that in our own country there could be no mistakes. Cheryl went so far as to order a large laurel wreath, and she declared that if the fight went the distance she'd be up there in the ring to hang it round my neck, and my brothers would chair me round the ring without waiting for the decision.

I never had the slightest doubt that I would become European Champion after the flogging Velensek took in that first fight, and the second meeting ran on very similar lines.

He didn't swarm in quite so much at Nottingham, no doubt remembering what he'd gone through before, but there were still times when I thought he wouldn't get off his stool for the next round. His courage was fantastic. I don't think I hurt him so much the second time, but he still got a good hiding and in the 13th round I cut him over his left eye. French referee Bernard Macot inspected the damage, but let him carry on, and for the rest of the fight I just kept pumping shots into his body and his ugly face.

This time there were no crooked officials, and both judges and the referee scored it well in my favour. Still, you've got to hand it to Velensek, the old bastard. They tell me he keeps a bar in Berlin and the way he soaked up the punishment I shouldn't think he has any trouble with any piss artists who come into his place!

Cheryl was as good as her word, and produced the giant laurel wreath. Unfortunately she didn't manage to get it round my neck before the decision was announced, but who cared? I was delighted. Not only was I European champion, but I had also redeemed the lie that had enabled my father to die a happy man.

He'd wanted me to win that European title more than anything else, and when I got back from Berlin after that poxy draw, I found that Dad was dying. I told him I'd beaten Velensek. He had a dream, and I made it come true. He died a few hours later believing me to be the champion, and as I watched him go I vowed that I would redeem those false words.

In that sense, beating Velensek was the most supremely satisfying moment in my life. My father was a good man, and I know that he's up there forgiving me for that bum steer.

CHAPTER FIFTEEN
The sherriff of Albuquerque

But life had to go on, and my sights were now set on world champion Bob Foster, that great big sherriff from Albuquerque. He was due to meet Vicente Rondon in Miami a few weeks later for the undisputed world title, and Sam Burns and I planned to be at the ringside to announce ourselves as the challenge for the winner.

Meanwhile I had to defend the European title against the Dutchman Jan Lubbers, and this was clearly a fight I couldn't afford to lose.

Lubbers kept a rifle range at an Amsterdam fairground, but there was no way I was going to let him bump me off! When we got in the ring he was no crack shot, and with a right uppercut in the eighth I nearly took his bleeding head off. He managed to stagger up at nine, but his legs had gone, and the referee completed the count. That was the end of that shooting match.

We turned our attention back to Foster. Albert Hall promoter Mike Barrett footed the bill for me to spy on Foster, but to tell the truth we didn't learn a lot. Foster stopped Rondon in the second round, and though Rondon had been the World Boxing Association's recognised champion, you didn't have to be an expert to see that he was shit scared. In fact he failed to reach the light-heavyweight limit of 11st 7lb so the whole thing turned into a bit of a fucking pantomime. Everyone knew that Foster would drop him – it was just a question of time. Foster stalked him round the ring for a few minutes and then hit him. Rondon just lay there looking as if someone had shot him with a bloody elephant rifle.

I was immediately introduced in the ring as a possible limey contender, but it was clear that nobody knew nor cared who the bleeding hell I was. 'You might not know me now,' I thought to myself, 'but you'll sodding well know me before I'm finished!'

Foster was due for another title defence before getting round to me, this time against Mike Quarry, whose older brother Jerry was fighting Muhammad Ali on the same bill in Las Vegas. At that time Ali had not regained the world title.

I watched on closed circuit television, and at first it seemed as if Mike Quarry wasn't doing too badly, moving in with good shots and giving the champion a little bit of bother. Until the fourth round. I reckon Foster simply got fed up with being pissed about, and I can honestly say that I've never seen a left hook delivered with such deadly effect. The sound Quarry made when he hit the deck was what you might expect if you threw a bag of cement from the top of the Post Office Tower. He didn't move a muscle.

Reg Gutteridge was doing the closed circuit commentary, and came out with 'This is the guy Chris Finnegan fancies his chances with!' That brought an almighty fucking laugh from the Hammersmith cinema audience. They didn't know that I was sitting there, and I remember thinking what a dirty lot of bastards they were.

I don't know how long it took them to scrape Quarry off the canvas, but I can honestly say that I didn't know where to put my face as we came out into the light where I was recognised. I felt a bit better when people started asking for my autograph – probably the same blokes that had been laughing about me a few minutes earlier – and I was determined that the last laugh would be with me.

It wasn't long before the good news came through that Harry Levene had secured the fight against Foster for Wembley on

September 26 1972. Training started at once. This was the most important fight of my life, and I was determined to be ready.

Two weeks later I had a bad day. First of all Cheryl told me that she was in the pudding club again – as if I didn't have enough on my hands – and then later the same day her mother dropped dead! It wasn't the best preparation I could have had, but if you're any sort of a fighter, you've got to shrug these things off. I had just turned 28, and couldn't afford to hang about, even if Foster was no chicken himself. Foster. I was beginning to hate the sound of his fucking name. Not that I was frightened. Everyone kept telling me what a murderous puncher he was, but I wasn't bothered. What really upset me was that people kept writing me off against this big black bean-pole. Idiots.

I trained like I'd never trained before. I ran so hard that Freddie Hill was calling me Arkle, and I reckon that the Guinness shares must have dropped a bit, because I didn't touch one for weeks. I almost forgot what one tasted like. (Almost!)

The day of the fight. I was the lowest of underdogs. I think every punter on the books was going for Foster. I never realised that so many people were concerned for my safety! Wally Bartleman's headline in the *Standard* was typical – 'Sorry, Chris, but this sherriff is sure to get you!' They were like a load of fucking vultures, just waiting for that left hook.

I've never really forgiven people for what they did to me before that fight. You can be the bravest bastard in the world, but all that frightening talk is like a sodding Chinese water torture, and I burnt up a lot of energy trying to ignore it.

Perhaps I didn't realise that at the time, though. I was on no survival course – I wanted to win. I knew Foster was good, but he was a human being, not some sort of god. I reckoned that the further the fight went, the better my chances would be. He'd been fed on a string of quick wins, and I didn't think his legs would fancy 15 rounds. And I was used to being the underdog. It had been like that in Mexico, and on a couple of occasions since. The Finnegan mob were right there behind me, plus that bloke upstairs, who I've always believed cares a little bit about me.

So as I bobbed and jogged down the aisle I was in an ice-cold mood. The fanfares were blazing away, and I didn't feel a bit like the geezer who's being led across the prison yard for a rope dance. The spotlight was on me and I was giving a nod and a wink to the punters as I made my way towards the ring surrounded by bloody great coppers. Then I spotted a finger in the sixth row who owed me a tenner. It was the balance on a wanker of a car I'd sold him, though why I thought about it at that moment I don't really know – nerves, I suppose.

As I drew level with him I stopped the procession and dived across and grabbed him by the neck.

'Here, what about that fucking cock and hen you owe me?'

He was speechless. Afterwards – and we've had a good few laughs about it since – he told his mates 'Fancy old Chrissie remembering that when he was on his way to such a fight. He must either be the bravest or the meanest bastard I've ever known!'

By the time the fight started I'd come to terms with myself. We were working to a plan, and I began by ducking and weaving – using the ring to keep out of trouble while he was burning up energy trying to get to me. In the early rounds he did hurt me a couple of times, but my determination took a lot of the pain away from the punches.

By the time we got to round five I was still there, and building up quite a lot of confidence. The crowd were beginning to catch on, too. They could see for themselves that I hadn't been destroyed, and they were looking for the miracle that everyone had said I needed to win.

As the rounds went by I came more into the fight, and with the crowd increasingly behind me I started standing toe-to-toe with Foster and trading punches. I started to catch him with one or two shots, and one in particular knocked his head back. I was hitting him everywhere – up the belly, in the balls, and anywhere I could catch the big black bastard.

But my legs were tiring. I'd used that old ring fairly well, and in the tenth round he caught me. A right hand landed on my chin, and I was straight over. I was hurt, all right, but more than that I was really getting tired. I watched Foster move over to a neutral corner with a smirky 'That's you finished' expression on his face. But he was wrong. I knew that after the compulsory eight count he would come in and try to finish me off, but if I was going to go, I determined that it would be in style. He rushed me as the referee moved away, but I stood there and threw everything I could at him, and by the end of the round I even had him back-pedalling.

The eleventh found me still very much alive and punching, although I wasn't kidding myself that I'd been ahead at any stage of the fight. By the time the 14th arrived, I was getting a bit wide-eyed and legless. As I sat on the stool my corner could see how

117

exhausted I was and tried to gee me up. Sam Burns stuck his head through the ropes.

'Look baby,' he said, 'the guy in the other corner is just as tired. When he saw you get up in the tenth he bloody nearly turned white!'

Freddie Hill was a bit more analytical. 'You can go out there and last the distance, or take the fight to him and give it everything you've got. That way you might get knocked out quite easily. Even if you keep on your bike you've put up a wonderful performance. Listen to the crowd screaming your name. What do you want to do, Chrissie boy?'

'Get out of my fucking way,' I replied as the bell went.

A minute later it was all over. He caught me with a left hook and I was straight on my arse. I can't remember the count, and I can't remember trying to get up, but they told me afterwards that I was really trying to get my legs to support me, and they just wouldn't. It was over.

The old sherriff had done me with his 12-bore, the rotten sod, and that was the end of that. What really got to me was that I'd been beaten by exhaustion more than the punching power of Foster. If only I hadn't been so tired.

Back in the dressing room there were congratulations from all corners. I'd been great in defeat, they said. Thanks a lot.

Wally Bartleman told me they'd offered a return. What did I think of it?

'Sure I'd like to fight him again,' I replied. 'What about to-morrow morning?'

To be fair to Foster, he was all there with the tributes

afterwards, and he meant what he said. Apparently I was the best-equipped of the eleven who had challenged him over four years, and he was big enough to admit that quite a few of my shots had hurt him.

There was the usual Finnegan-style celebration when we got back home. Anyone would have thought that I'd won the bleeding title! We went on all through the night, and I soon got that Guinness flavour right back in my gills. The only thing Cheryl and I didn't take much part in was the dancing, because I was knackered, and she was up the duff!

On reflection we hadn't done too badly. I almost went the distance for one thing. If I'd sploshed out early on I reckon Cheryl would have had a premature birth on her hands at the ringside — me laying spark out in the ring and her in a similar position in the front row!

CHAPTER SIXTEEN
Pickle-head

It was a fight which found me in great demand for all sorts of functions, and we started getting plenty of work. But only six weeks later the European Boxing Union dropped a bombshell. They ordered me to defend my European title against the German, Rudi Schmidtke, at Wembley, in the same ring in which I'd fought my heart out against Foster. There was no doubt that the Foster fight had taken a lot out of me. In fact when the sherriff heard that I had been forced to fight again after such a short time he didn't believe it. Then he got quite angry and suggested that the people who were kicking me into the ring so soon should be put up against a wall and shot. In his opinion I needed at least six months' rest.

But there was no getting out of it, short of being stripped of the title, and the fight had to go on. This was in 1972, a year in which I had already had a tremendous second fight with Velensek, a successful defence against Lubbers, and the stamina-sapping affair with Foster. And there had been two other fights thrown in for good measure. Everyone was expecting another marvellous performance from me, but I was a long way under par, and the old sparkle was missing. The meeting with the old sherriff had taken its toll.

To cap it all, this Schmidtke geezer was no slouch. He had won all but four of his pro fights, and had twice beaten Conny Velensek – the first time in four rounds. I had my work cut out, all right.

After ten rounds my corner told me that I was ahead on points, which is always nice to know, and all I had to do was stay on my feet to keep the title. That's where I came unstuck – I didn't stay on my feet. In the 11th the kraut swung a right-hand chopping

121

punch and caught me right on the hooter. The old conk opened up right down the middle, just like a split walnut, and I've still got the scar to prove it.

I couldn't see a thing. Blood was everywhere. It was probably the biggest mess since Henry Cooper got done by Cassius Clay. I went to the corner at the end of the round, and Freddie Hill smacked the old adrenalin on it to try and stop the bleeding. He asked me how I felt about going out for the 12th. I thought I'd be OK if I could get the blood out of my eyes, but though Freddie did his best, it was clear that he couldn't stop such a cut from bleeding.

I went out again, but the old kraut came steaming in and the next thing I knew my nose was streaming again, and both eyes were bunged up with blood. I tucked myself into a little ball with both gloves covering my face, taking a swipe whenever I thought Schmidtke was in range. But the referee knew that I couldn't see anything, and it was only a few moments before he stopped the fight. That was my European title up the pictures.

It was a terrible disappointment, of course, but I'm not unused to getting over these things, and it wasn't long before I was defending the British and Commonwealth titles against Welshman Roy John – again at Wembley. I was beginning to feel like a regular tenant. That particular fight wasn't much to shout about, and I had no trouble keeping both titles on a points decision.

It was a double-header bill at the Empire Pool that night. All of a sudden some geezer called John Conteh had got into the fucking action, and he was challenging Schmidtke for my old European title. If anyone should have been fighting the German, it was me, but they bunged in this cheeky bastard Conteh, who'd been boiled down from heavyweight to light-heavy – a weight at which he'd never fought as a pro.

Still, that's how they work and that's how it had to be. Conteh did Schmidtke in 12 rounds, and then the plan they'd all been working on became apparent. The idea was to match me with Conteh with all three titles going into the hat. We were assured that we were going to make a lot of dough. It was a natural match, I suppose, but I'd seen John fight and approached my meeting with him without any real concern.

We had never met as amateurs, but had done some sparring together as pros. Now everyone was hailing him as the next world champion, but I could recall finding him fairly easy to hit. I was under-dog again, but all that did was give me extra incentive to prove a few berks wrong.

My preparation was as rigorous as ever, for that Freddie Hill is a bleeding hard taskmaster whether you're fighting for a title or are down the bill. He'll stand no fucking about up at the Craven Arms, and whenever Kevin or I turned up late or missed a session, he'd tell us to piss off out of it.

He's a sadist. He likes making people suffer. But gawd knows where I would have been without him. In training for Conteh we concentrated on pressuring – taking the fight to him – because we reckoned he might not be too strong at the weight. After all, it was only his second fight as a light-heavy. It would be a very hard fight whatever happened, but there was a real chance that he would blow out. Schmidtke had never put him under the sort of pressure that would show up any weakness where weight was concerned.

Mind you, other people were airing their doubts about me. It

123

had been a hard year, and my fight against Lubbers – eight rounds – had been the shortest. And I was paying the penalty in more ways than one. With four title fights in one year, the fucking tax man was always standing on my doorstep!

One of these days they might come round to spreading a boxer's earnings over several years, like they do in the theatre, but as it stands now top fighters are left with a pissing two bob in the pound after that berk has been down their pockets.

But this fight with Conteh was going to ease the financial cramp. There was talk of Foster quitting the world crown, and with John and me ranked three and four in the world the way could be open for a bonanza. Conteh was within a few days of his 21st birthday, and I was in my 30th year, so no wonder they were talking about Finnegan's last stand. The famous Conteh right hand would get me, they were saying. But it didn't go that way.

It was a great fight all right – reckoned to be one of the best light-heavyweight wars for years – and Harry Levene certainly had a sell-out on his hands that night in May 1973. For ten rounds it was anybody's fight, although most had Conteh slightly ahead on their cards. But I felt that he was getting a bit frustrated. He hadn't knocked me over, and he wasn't very happy about it. Most of his opponents had finished on the deck well before that, and I was quite happy because I knew I had the stamina to see it through.

Then, in the tenth, Conteh got the break he was looking for – in more ways than one. They called it a clash of heads, but there is no doubt that it was a butt. He stuck his nut right down across my eyebrow, the skin above the right eye split, and the blood came cascading down my face.

The significance of this wasn't lost on Conteh. His corner obviously advised him that now was the time to put me away, and he came out for the next round like a fucking lunatic. But I wasn't that easy. I made him go all the way, with the terrible handicap of my right eye being bunged up with blood. The only trouble is that to win in that situation you've got to have a big dig – like 'Enery's hammer – to give yourself a chance of winning, and I've always been a journeyman rather than a whacker.

I went on matching him punch for punch right up to the bell. I even had his gumshield out at one point. The only thing the fight lacked was a knock-down, and that tenth-round butt veered the fight in his direction. When referee Sid Nathan lifted Conteh's fork at the end I couldn't argue with the decision. He had scored more points than me.

Someone asked me whether Conteh's punching had given me any trouble, and I had to admit that he could hurt quite a bit, but as far as trouble was concerned it was fuck all compared with what I might expect from the missus when we got home! I'd done my two titles, and Johnny boy was holding a three flush and chasing after that world crown. The only consolation came in the words of Sam Burns, who reckoned that the audience reaction at the end – they had loved every minute of it – would ensure a return by public demand.

In the meantime I went home for some booze. About two weeks before the fight Cheryl had found a wicker basket on the doorstep with three bottles of champagne in it. At the time I was staying, as I always did during the final stages of training, at Freddie Hill's home in Camberwell Green. He used to watch me like a bleeding hawk, never letting me out of his sight.

Cheryl telephoned to thank me for the nice gesture and to say how much she was missing me.

'What nice gesture?' I asked.

'The three bottles of champagne in the wicker basket on the doorstep,' she replied.

'You must be out of your sodding mind,' I said. 'I might send a crate of Guinness round, but champagne?'

We never did find out who sent it, but if there's any more where that came from, I'd be only too glad to have it! It was a very popular ingredient in the knees-up after the Conteh fight, but it didn't last long!

The time had come for a real long rest and a holiday. I was looking forward to it like a kid, but even when we were away I always kept myself in trim with a bit of running. If you don't do that, especially at my age, you find it all the harder to get back into trim when the time comes.

It was almost six months before my name appeared on another bill. It was Wembley again, and I was lined up to figure in a fight supporting Conteh's meeting with Mike Quarry, who had been pole-axed by Foster a year earlier. I must admit that I found it a bit humiliating being down the card, and people were starting to talk again about the beginning of the end for Chris Finnegan. I was down to meet some unknown yank.

Then, ho, ho, what do you know? Only a few days before the show Conteh pulled out. And I know why. I reckon that head of his wasn't in sufficiently good condition. To tell the truth I think he got it stuck in a fucking gherkin jar. I reckon he spends his time between fights with his head in among the gherkins and pickled onions to toughen it up.

So his loaf wasn't properly pickled, and they stuck me in there against Quarry. I reckon they thought I would soften up the Yank for Conteh, in much the same way that I'd taken the starch out of Schmidtke. I hadn't fought for six months, and had no titles, but I had had a good rest, and was feeling nice and strong. Most of the crowd, apart from my loyal supporters, thought I was washed up over the top, with about two quick pay-days left and then back to the bricklayer's monkey.

My ten-rounder against Quarry on November 13 had them thinking again. I dominated that fight from start to finish, and Quarry hardly laid a glove on me. Against Foster he had done quite well until the lights went out, but I never let him get near me. I took the fight to him all the time, and really pissed on him for ten rounds for one of the easiest wins I've ever had.

Quarry was still highly rated in the States, so I said to myself, 'Chrissie boy, this is where you can have another go at old pickle-head!' And I was right, although it took until the following May before we got down to business for a second time.

After Quarry I had another good rest before thinking about getting my three titles back. At the back of my mind all this time was that big black sherriff from Albuquerque. If only I could get that Bob Foster back in the ring. But Conteh came first.

I sat down with Cheryl and we talked the whole business over. There's not much she doesn't know about the fight business, so we put our heads together – her head's much nicer than Conteh's –

and we tried to plan how to avoid head injury. The trouble is that I can never be serious for long, and the old woman didn't think much of my idea of writing to the British Boxing Board of Control asking if I could enter the ring wearing a crash helmet!

But work down at the Craven Arms gym was serious enough, especially with Freddie Hill standing behind me. We all knew that Conteh was going well – he had the words 'King John' inscribed on the back of his sequined dressing gown for the world title fight hullabaloo build-up, with 'Man of Destiny' written underneath it in French so that ignorant twerps like me couldn't understand it.

I was determined to settle his destiny there and then. I don't think I ever went to a fight feeling fitter or more confident that it was going to be my big night. They tell me that I looked a bit tense during the preliminaries, with none of the usual nodding and winking to my supporters at the ringside. This is probably true, but it was a good sign. It showed that deep down inside there was hate boiling up. And hate, provided it's controlled, it a great asset to a fighter.

Despite what anyone might say to the contrary, I took the first five rounds, no bother. The old jab was going well, and I remember seeing a photo afterwards that showed Conteh's face like a deflated football as I caught him with a right hook that clearly shook him.

In the sixth he turned on a bit of pressure, but that's only because he knew he had to do a fucking sight better if he was going to hold on to his titles and get that world shot.

But did he fight with his fists in order to win? Did he bloody hell. He came wading in with his loaf going like a good'un. He was going barmy, and I already had a slight nick over each eye. Then he came charging in again and I caught the full force of his loaf. I pulled away and the blood was streaming down my face. I wasn't sure exactly where the cut was, but referee Roland Dakin took the view that it was around the right eye.

When I got back to my corner Freddie Hill wiped the blood away, and there was a three-inch gash on my scalp, high up over my right ear where the parting is. How the hell can a cut like that be caused by a boxing glove? Every time I run a comb through my hair today I can still see the scar.

The referee didn't give me a chance, and stopped the fight straight away. You can imagine how I felt. I stayed long enough to see Conteh booed out of the ring. At the end of the fifth he'd thrown half a dozen punches after the bell, which turned the crowd against him, and now this had to happen.

The crowd were throwing anything they could lay their hands on at Conteh, and my old woman was going stark raving mad, calling him every name under the sun.

Later I watched an unedited film of the fight, and the thing that struck me most was not his headwork but the fact that between each round his corner was giving him shit, telling him that he had to work a lot harder for his win. I was doing well, smothering him with right jabs, and between me and his corner I reckon he was getting mad.

To be fair to the referee it did seem, as the blood ran through my eyebrow, that I'd been cut over the eye, but the usual procedure in these cases is for the referee to walk you to your corner and get the second to wipe the blood away, so that the wound can be in-

129

spected. They might even call up the quack for an inspection. Fuck knows what happened this time. Dakin just decided to stop the affair, and even as he was leading me to my corner Conteh was still tossing shots at me.

Freddie would have plugged that injury with vaseline had the referee given him a chance, but Dakin just scrubbed me without having a close look at the damage and Conteh started prancing and leaping round the ring like a madman when he realised he'd got the verdict for a second time.

Most of the journalists present said afterwards that it was a matter of conjecture which way the fight would have gone but for Conteh's head. Nonsense. I was Conteh's guv'nor that night so far as sharpness and boxing were concerned, and that's what it's all about.

I hate to think what would have happened if my old woman or any of my brothers had got to Conteh that night. She was waving her handbag about, and I reckon Conteh must have been shitting himself in case she got to grips with him. His head wouldn't have done him any good then, because she would have got the butt in first! I know – I've had some of it!

CHAPTER SEVENTEEN

Gypsy Johnny and the Lonsdale Belt

When all the fuss had died down, I was back to square one. The cry 'Finnegan's finished' went up again, and it really did begin to look as if there might not be a lot left for the monkey kid.

It was a further four-and-a-half months before I got back in action, with a couple of bread and butter fights in which I got points decisions against Harold Richardson and Victor Attivor. There was one more event which didn't make 1974 a very happy year for me – on October 1 at Wembley. Conteh became world champion by outscoring Jorge Ahumada. Foster had been stripped of his title for refusing to fight Conteh. I reckon the old sherriff must have heard what a nutter Johnny was!

By the middle of 1975 I was sitting around scratching my balls and wondering what to do next when it was suddenly announced that Conteh had given up the British light-heavyweight title and I'd been named to meet Johnny Frankham for the crumbs old pickle-head had brushed off the table.

I knew all about gypsy John. I'd boxed him twice as an amateur, once in the ABA championships at Stanmore and once on a hotel dinner show. They were both fairly close affairs, and I knew that John was a crafty and clever bastard. I'd got the points decisions both times, and knew that he was likely to tire in the latter stages, probably because he wasn't very enthusiastic about training.

I don't suppose Jonto would be prepared to admit it, but I practically stopped him at Stanmore. I was thumping him on the ropes and the referee was just beginning to lead him away when the bell went, so he was allowed to return to his corner without interference.

I suppose I had to be grateful that old pickle-head had given me the chance to get back by vacating the British title, and I was delighted that Gyppo Frankham was the man I had to beat. We're similar in many ways – always ready with a wisecrack, a bit irresponsible at times, and very fond of drinking.

We both know a bit about boxing, too, and can promote ourselves, so when this first professional meeting between us came along they probably wondered whether to put it on at Wembley, the Albert Hall, or the bleeding Palladium! All the seats were sure to sell wherever it was, and promoter Mike Barrett had a grin as wide as a tabby-cat's when he quickly sold out the Albert Hall.

I went to the weigh-in determined not to be outdone by Frankham's gypsy mob, which equals my own in noise and numbers. I wore a pair of earrings, a polka-dot scarf, and a load of pegs round my shoulders, and Johnny and his crowd took it pretty well. There's no malice between us, but I would stress that contrary to popular opinion, we're not exactly bosom pals, either. I think the Frankhams kept the pegs as a souvenir.

But when the bell sounds the joking finishes and the meanness in every man comes out. So it was for Frankham and me. Frankham had been known to clown about in some of his fights, but like me he was dead serious when the real chips were down. We both wanted that title and the cash that went with it quite badly.

It started as a great fight. I forced it all the way, but Frankham was his usual cute self, was counterpunching well, and ignored my efforts to get him to come in close. So I thought I'd try a change of tactics. I wanted to get him playing about a bit, and break his concentration, so I put in an Ali shuffle and gave him the old come-on

132

signal.

That did it. Harry Gibbs stopped the fight and gave me a right bollocking. Any more antics like that, and I would be slung out! I just wondered how old Harry would get on if he was refereeing an Ali fight. Perhaps he was just shitting me. I've often wished I'd done it again to see what would have happened!

The crowd were enjoying every minute of it. Both sets of supporters were screaming their heads off, creating an atmosphere that you all too rarely see on the big fight scene these days.

Then, during the sixth round, Frankham's nut opened me up over the left eye. I always seem to be claiming this, but it's absolutely true. He'd done a Conteh on me. And when your opponent sees the blood oozing, it brings him to life like a shark on the scent of blood, and Frankham was no exception.

When I went back to my corner at the end of the round, Harry Gibbs came over to have a look at the injury, and Freddie Hill wasn't slow to tell him what he thought. There was a sharp exchange of words between them, but Gibbs didn't reckon he'd stop the fight, which was a relief. I suppose Harry might have got the hump over that bit of verbal from my chief second, and it might not have done me any good. I wasn't saying anything. I just sat there drinking my own blood.

The fight went on for the full 15 bloody bruising battering rounds, and before the end Frankham was also cut – over both eyes. I'll give Johnny credit – he stuck to his task of staying out of trouble and counter-punching well, and I reckon we both thought we'd done enough to win. I certainly did. Frankham was so confident that when the bell went at the end, he walked over to Gibbs and held his hand out. Gibbs lifted it!

Well, it might have been close, I'll grant you that, but I was sure I'd won. My supporters felt the same way, and there were more fights outside the ring that night than in it! Bottles were flying everywhere, and I was thankful that no-one got badly hurt – particularly as my old woman was in the middle of it. She'd taken it into her head to get into the ring and have a go at Harry Gibbs. He can thank his lucky stars she didn't make it, because I wouldn't fancy his chances with her. Not only that, but we would have been right in the shit if she'd clouted him!

The next day was Derby day, and when we found that Frankham and his jolly gypsies were going to be at Epsom, as indeed was our mob, the signals appeared to be up for another confrontation. But before that came the usual little drink back home.

We were right brassed off about the decision – Frankham had appparently made it by half-a-point – and we didn't stop drinking till four in the morning. The next thing I knew it was half past nine, and the bloody coach was waiting outside our front door. It was full of the Finnegan clan on their way to the Derby, and they were waiting for me and the missus to join them. You can imagine what a state I was in. Fifteen bloody hard rounds, cut and bruised all over, pissed as a rat, and with no sleep to speak of!

There was even some booze on the coach, and as soon as we got to Epsom I was straight in the beer tents for a hair from the dog . . .

Then I remembered. I'd agreed to do a television broadcast from Epsom, and Frankham was supposed to be on the same little show. This would be funny. I made my way to the television enclosure, and found that Frankham was already there with his missus. He was being a complete gentleman this time. The bastard was obviously sober, and had had a good night's kip.

As champion, Frankham was asked to say his piece first, and naturally he didn't think there was any doubt about the decision. Bill Grundy was the interviewer, and what with Grundy winning the race and me pissed out of mind, it was beginning to look like Monty Python's Flying Circus by the time I managed to get my piece in. Not a very clever piece of stage management on my part, that.

When the dust had settled, I realised that I had to concentrate on getting Frankham back in the ring. There was no way that the matter could be allowed to rest after such a controversial decision, and I reckon that Mike Barrett was already banking on another sell-out. The return was duly fixed for October 14 1975, and it was the general opinion that in no way could the second clash be as thrilling as the first. Over the years this has usually proved to be the case with return fights, and it wasn't surprising that most critics considered that Frankham would win again, and this time a lot more easily.

I don't think I've ever been more ready for a fight. I was so fit and sharp in training that my mind went back to the 1968 Olympics, and so confident was I that for the first time I allowed my daughter Pearl to come to the Albert Hall and watch me fight. She was 12 years old, and I think her presence led to my old woman adopting a far lower key than she had in the first fight. In fact she only really got any steam up in the 12th round, when it looked as if I might have Frankham going.

By the time this fight came around I reckoned I knew all there was to know about Frankham. He was as slippery as a jellied eel. I went to the television studio to watch the film of the first fight over and over again, and I could see where I'd been making my mistakes. I'd been too anxious the first time round in taking the fight to Frankham and I had probably walked into more shots than were healthy for me.

Kevin came to the studios with me to look at the re-runs. He's got a pretty shrewd boxing brain and we learned a lot from what we saw. By the end of the session we had my plan of attack worked out. Frankham had been saying that he was like a dog with a bone – there was no way that he was going to give it up. What he didn't realise was that when a bigger and better dog comes along, you've got to hand it over. And so it proved.

The Frankham mob who had been creeping round the ringside trying to lay wagers on their man were making their usual row, but by about half way they'd gone awfully quiet. And long before the end they'd completely finished, although most people thought this second fight was just as good as the first.

But referee Wally Thom, like me a southpaw in his day, didn't mess about. He scored it 149–146$\frac{1}{2}$ – seven rounds to me, two to Frankham, and six even. Not bad for an old drunk of 31. I'd won a Lonsdale belt outright in my twelfth championship fight. My superior staying power saw me through.

I can now reveal that Thom, a former welterweight champion who'd been a bloody good man in his day, gave me a couple of useful points when he came to give his instructions in the dressing room before the fight.

He said he wanted a good clean fight with no head butts and all that old mularkey, but added that I must keep my cool. I had been a pro long enough to size up a situation, and if I lost my head I would probably lose the fight. I pondered on what were undoubtedly wise words.

Those words paid off well, and I think someone must have said the same thing to the blonde bomber, because she had a quiet evening, and for once I did it my way.

We had our usual couple of drinks when we got home, and people were starting to talk about how old pickle-head should settle the various differences he was having with people at the time, and enjoy a world title fight bonanza with me. My mind was also going back to old Mate Parlov of Yugoslavia, who I'd seen off in the Olympics. He'd gone on to win the next Olympic title before turning pro, and was now among the leading European cruisers, having won all his fights. Perhaps we might catch up with each other again.

But it was decided that first of all I had to defend my British title against Roy John, who I had met and well outpointed for the British and Commonwealth crowns in 1973. I didn't think that would be a severe obstacle, and reckoned that I'd be putting myself on easy street so far as my fight earning potential was concerned.

But, of course, it doesn't pay to count your chickens before they're hatched.

CHAPTER EIGHTEEN
The eye

Training started going well for the title defence. Freddie Hill was cracking the fucking whip down at the gym and expressed himself well satisfied with the way things were going.

Then came the first scare. My hand started hurting, but I reckoned that it would be a short-term problem and invited the Press down to the gym to watch me work out. Most of them reckoned that I'd never looked better, so that was one problem on the way out.

Then one day I became conscious of blurred vision in my right eye. At first I thought I'd caught a chill. It had happened before. It would clear up in a day or two. I decided to keep it to myself. After a couple of days I started getting flashes across the eye, and that really worried me. Perhaps, I told myself, I'd got a thumb in my eye during sparring. It would clear up. It was bound to.

One night Kevin was driving me home from training – I'd managed to accumulate a three-year lay-off due to the old plastic bag routine – and he made some remark about the car in front. That did it. I couldn't see any bleeding car! Kevin was as shocked as I was. As I leaned forward and peered into the darkness I could just about make out the shape of a car in front, but I couldn't tell you what sort of car it was.

I did my roadwork next morning, and a bit of shadow boxing, but things weren't getting any better, and in the end I had to tell Cheryl.

The trouble was that I still wasn't sure what to say. You always try and kid yourself that things aren't as bad as they seem, but sometimes you're wrong. I told Cheryl that I was experiencing some trouble with the eye, but also told her that it was probably

139

the effect of a thumb in the eye in sparring, or a chill. Only a doctor could tell for sure, and I had a visit to the quack lined up because of my forthcoming fight.

A promoter will always insure himself when he puts on a boxing show. After all, if one of the big names on the bill pulls out at the last minute, for whatever reason, the promoter's in dead stuck, and stands to lose a fortune. But the insurance companies always demand that the fighters are certified as being medically fit before they will issue a policy, and so off I went to the local quack – a feller I've known for a number of years. He'd given me a pretty good going over about three months previously, and I asked him for another check for the sake of Mike Barrett's insurance.

As I sat in the waiting room I found myself subconsciously giving myself an eye test by covering one eye and then trying to read the notices on the wall – 'Smoking is bad for you', 'Please try and make requests for a home call before 10 a.m.' and all that business. My eye was no better, and still I was thinking of all the little things that could be causing the trouble.

When I got in to see the doc, he gave me a thorough check – chest, heart, legs, arms – but I knew before he started that he'd find nothing wrong there. But he didn't give me an eye test, even though he had one of those charts hanging on the wall. All he did was shine a light in my eyes – I believe they call it an opthalmoscope – and have a good squint round. It didn't take him long to issue a certificate of fitness to fight, and so I went off to the gymnasium to get on with the training. I was banging away doing ten rounds each session with Johnny Wall and my brother Kevin – they're both good punchers. I took quite a few shots on the head,

140

and after a while I realised that my vision was getting much worse. I was still fooling myself that as I'd been passed fit there couldn't be much wrong with me, but the worry just nagged and nagged at me until eventually I convinced myself that I'd seen a general practitioner – he wasn't an eye specialist.

The moment of truth came next morning when I was doing some roadwork. I've always been good at running, but on this morning my eye was worse than ever, and I started losing my equilibrium. I was stumbling all over the place and found it increasingly hard to keep my balance. I'd been doing about six miles on the road each morning, and had never had trouble like this before. I enjoyed galloping – I even used to look forward to it – but now I began to realise that if I couldn't keep my balance in this situation, how the hell was I going to stand up in a ring?

The only thing to do was to go back to the doctor straight away. When I arrived at the surgery, he was rather surprised to see me. By this time I was blind in my right eye, and I told him just that. Out came the opthalmoscope again, and this time he spent so long crouched over me I reckon he must have worn the bleeding battery out. Eventually he straightened up.

'I think you know what I'm looking for, Chris,' he said. 'I'm trying to discover if there's any sign of what, in your trade, is called a detached retina.'

That shook me, but I was somewhat reassured when he added that he couldn't actually see any relevant symptoms. I told him that I couldn't see objects on the far side of the room, and that at the best of times I could only see the tops of objects. I could see he was concerned. As I've said, I knew the bloke quite well, and he knew me well enough to realise that I didn't fuck about where my health was concerned.

He thought for a few moments, and then said that he'd like me to see an eye specialist in Windsor. I could only go as a private patient if I wanted to do this quickly, but the cost was the last thing I was worried about. Sod the expense. My eyes were an important part of my trade, and even though I would have faced Roy John with one eye, I willingly agreed to see this man.

The doc promised to make the appointment for me, so I went home to wait for his call. About four in the afternoon he telephoned to say that he had been lucky enough to get me in to see this geezer that very same evening. The trouble was that I was about to leave for the gym in Lavender Hill, so the evening was a bit inconvenient. The fight was only about ten days off, and I knew what would happen if I rang and told Freddie Hill that I wasn't coming in that evening. When it comes to pre-fight training, Freddie is a sodding animal, and won't listen to any excuses. If I told him my eyes were bad I knew what he'd think. I'd been out on the piss. I could hardly stand up. Any excuse. How the fucking hell did I expect to beat Roy John if I was fucking well pissed? Who ever won big fights without training seriously? You're a cunt, Finnegan, what are you?

I was dreading it, but I knew that the truth would out in the end, and I was telling the truth, so I picked up the phone. He listened to what I had to say, and made it quite clear that he didn't believe a word of it. He said everything I expected him to say, and then he tried to persuade me that any symptoms I might be having were down to pre-fight nerves. It's true that as a fight approaches you start to get a lot of funny aches and pains, whereas as soon as the fight is over, you're as fit as an Aspro, and would willingly tackle the world.

But I kept on at him, and eventually he subdued himself a bit and agreed to let me go and see this doctor, who, after all, had been kind enough to fit me in at such short notice. That night we had all arranged to go and see a play called *Johnny Boxer* after training, and consequently Cheryl had fixed up an appointment with the hairdresser to get her roots tinted. After all, she is the champion's wife, so she's got to look the part. We couldn't have her sitting in the front stalls with her roots a different colour from the rest of her hair, could we?

So Kevin's wife, Marilyn, agreed to run me up to the doc at Windsor while Goldilocks got herself spruced up. Kevin and Marilyn were both going to see the play with us, and everyone was looking forward to a good old piss-up afterwards.

I sat in the waiting room at Windsor for a few minutes – you don't have to wait long when you're paying for it – and had a glance at the books and magazines that were scattered about. I couldn't see a bloody thing with my right eye by this time, and I found myself getting nervous as the moment of truth approached.

When I went in to the doc's room, it was like something out of science fiction, with all sorts of wierd and wonderful gadgets spread about the place. There was one with a harness for the head, and a rest for the chin, and the doc asked me to sit there, with my head held in place by straps. He explained that he would be introducing lines of white light into my vision from the sides, and I was to indicate the moment I spotted them.

I thought this would be a piece of cake, because my reactions have always been needle sharp, and I lived on speed. I might not carry a heavy punch, but I could usually hit a bloke about six times before he could lay a glove on me.

So my good eye was covered, and we began. As soon as I spotted the line, I would shout 'Got it!' and he started firing them at me from all angles. I thought I was doing well. When he'd had enough I removed my head from the contraption, and asked him 'How did I do?' I fully expected him to say 'Very well'. He didn't.

He looked me straight in the eye and said 'Mr Finnegan, I must be very frank with you. Your performance was very poor – very poor indeed. I have to tell you that you've got a detached retina, and I don't think you fully realise what that means.'

He took me over to his desk and drew a diagram for me, fully explaining what a detached retina was. He made the situation very clear indeed. As far as I could tell the bloody retina was hanging on its last thread.

It was just like being kicked in the bollocks. I had never dreamt that anything like this could happen to me. I was Chris Finnegan, the superfit athlete with a heartbeat and condition that had astounded the doctors before I left for Mexico. The doctor's voice seemed to be miles away as he told me that I had to go straight to hospital for immediate surgery.

I pleaded with him to give me a couple of days to sort myself out. I had never had an operation in my life, and the prospect terrified me. I was shaking with fear. I had to have time to compose myself.

He just looked at me and quietly said, 'I don't think you realise just how serious the condition is – you could be blind within 24 hours just by walking about.'

By this time I knew that it was useless to think of fighting, but I was still trying to stall for time. I don't really know why. I think I fancied a drink! I told the doctor what was going through my mind. I just wanted a drink or two to ease the shock, but his face remained stony blank.

'There is only a fifty-fifty chance of saving the eye as it is,' he declared, 'and if we are to succeed, we must operate as soon as possible. I don't want to alarm you unnecessarily, but there is a good chance that your other eye will go the same way.'

That was it. My bottle went straight away. It had never happened to me in a fight, but it had happened now. When I walked out of that surgery I was in a daze, and my arsehole had been left behind. Marilyn was waiting for me, and she could see the tears welling up in my eyes.

I don't think we said above a dozen words as we drove the short distance to the hospital in Windsor, and by the time Cheryl arrived to see me I was in bed. I just looked at her. I didn't really feel like pouring out all my troubles to her, even though she is my missus. In any case, I was almost feeling too pissed off to talk to anyone. I had taken a blow far harder than any fight opponent had ever given me – including Bob Foster – and it showed. But I couldn't hide much from Cheryl – she knows me far too well for that. We just looked for a few seconds, and then we were crying together.

I don't think I had any sleep at all that night. It was like a waking nightmare, and now that I look back on it I find it very hard to remember anything about it. When morning came it wasn't long before I was surrounded by a crowd of merchants who I discovered later were headed by a wonderful surgeon called Kamski, who was later to operate on me.

The examination began all over again, with the flashing lights in my eyes and all the whispering going on. I began to feel like a fucking animal on show in a zoo. Then came the preparation for the operation. Talk about drying out for a fucking fight. They starved me all day, and by the end of it my guts felt as though they'd been hung out to dry.

Then they bleeding well decided that they didn't have the laser gun that was essential to the operation in Windsor, so the operation was to be postponed for 48 hours and performed in the Moorfields Eye Hospital in Holborn. I got a bit agitated when I heard this news, and the nurses had a job persuading me to keep my head still. They were afraid I might do the surgeon out of a job. Eventually they convinced me that everything was for the good, and would I like an ambulance to take me to London?

I didn't want any sodding ambulance – Cheryl could drive me in our car, thank you very much. Mind you, there was an ulterior motive – we didn't go straight to Moorfields! Instead, we dropped in at Manzi's fish restaurant near Leicester Square for some grub. I was still hungry and thirsty from the previous day's experience, and got stuck in to a huge bloody sole with great relish, washing it down with lager. During the meal a waiter came over and said that he'd just heard on the radio that I was in Moorfields, about to undergo an operation.

'Not yet, baby,' I told him, 'but it won't be long!' An hour later I waddled into the hospital and asked for the Bernhard Baron ward, where I was ordered into bed right away. They gave me a sedative injection, and I was more worried about that needle than the surgeon's knife, but it did relax me, and a couple of hours later they wheeled me out of the ward, along the corridor, and into what looked like a kitchen. I discovered that it was the anaesthetic room, which adjoins the main theatre, and it was here that I would be knocked out.

They looked like a bunch of men from Mars, wandering about in their gowns and masks, but I found myself wondering whether I would ever see my wife and kids again. I think that if it hadn't been for that pre-med injection, I would have been in an awful state.

The last thing I remember was a nurse saying, 'This won't hurt, Mr Finnegan,' and that was that. I was gone – a cleaner and swifter job than ever old pickle-head or Foster accomplished.

The next thing I knew, I was coming out of a mist, and Cheryl was sitting by the bedside. I could see her! I could see her! I could have cried with joy. But what I didn't know then was that I was coming round for a second time. I had earlier recovered consciousness and started struggling to get out of bed, declaring my intention of going home to see the wife and kids! The fact that Cheryl had been trying to get me back into bed hadn't got through to me. So they'd had to take the needle out for a second dose, and away I went for another couple of hours. Now I was in a much calmer frame of mind.

When I got Cheryl properly back in focus with my good eye – and they later told me that it was normal in every respect – I realised for the first time what sight really means. I can't possibly describe what it felt like to still be able to see – maybe only a little at first, but still to see.

Before long my hands drifted round behind the locker at the bedside, and there was a crate of Guinness! I thought to myself, 'Wait until they come round with that bleeding Horlicks – it's going straight out the window!'

CHAPTER NINETEEN
The search ends

I received some wonderful messages of encouragement and good wishes during the next few days, as well as a steady supply of Guinness! There were also visits from a good many people – both inside and outside boxing – who convinced me that Chris Finnegan still had a lot to live for.

It wasn't easy. The sight of my right eye had more or less gone – though thank God the other one was OK – and my head ached nearly all the time, but I was determined not to let people down. My career inside the ring might be over, but there was still a lot to fight for outside the ring.

There are people who reckon that now I'm cursing boxing – blaming some of the punishment I took for what happened to my eye, but it simply isn't true. I'm proud of the fight business and the little part I played in its history. No-one will ever hear me knocking it, and if I hear anyone running it down in my hearing, they'll soon find out what sort of a fucking punch I can still land on their nose.

I know I haven't always been everyone's cup of tea. Rags to riches and back again might well describe my life. But I've always been honest with everyone – except perhaps myself – and now I've got no grudges.

There was a time – probably right up until this eye business – when I had a chip on my shoulder. We never had any money when I was a kid, and all my young life I looked at people who had more than me and marvelled at the wonderful time they were having. I was jealous, and I wanted the same. It was a resentment that went right back to those sports days in Cowley when the other kids would turn up in smart, clean sports gear, and we would just roll up our jeans and run in bare feet. I seemed to miss the most important fact at the time – they had more money, but the Finnegans were winning the races! But nevertheless, I was jealous.

Secretly, I always longed for the good things. And then, almost overnight, I was a star. 'Right', I thought. 'This is it! This is where I join the good-time club!' But, to my great surprise, I found it wasn't easy. I was searching for something – that magic ingredient that would give me a good time – and I couldn't find it anywhere. I thought that a certain type of people would help me to have a good time, or that certain clubs and functions that were now open to me would hold the secret.

What a berk I was – pissing my money away in an effort to enjoy myself, with no thought for the consequences. And, of course, it all proved a dismal failure, and now I stand stripped of all pretence.

But at least I found what I was looking for – that contentment and happiness that I thought only money could buy. It exists within my home. I'd been running around all over the place looking for it, and coming home more often than not too pissed to recognise it when I saw it.

It's my wife – the real champ of the family – my two daughters, and my home. It's with them that I finally discovered the happiness and sense of security that I had stupidly passed up. It is said that there are none so blind who won't see, and that's a saying that can certainly be applied to me.

The blow that came perilously near to preventing me ever seeing the faces of those I so dearly love has in fact been the eye-opener to the truth that for so long I refused to face up to.

Epilogue

Now that my fighting days are over, I'm quite aware that there will be some people only too ready to predict that 'Finnegan will soon hit the slide', and I can't deny that my track record warrants such a prophecy. But if you look closely at my form you'll discover that when I set my mind on something, I'm a mighty difficult guy to push off course. And I'm determined to stay away from that slide!

I've had the laugh on my detractors before, and I'm certain that I'll have it again. Although I spent a lot of the money that I earned during my fighting career, I've got a few bob left, and I won't be seen squandering whatever else I earn in the future. I was overwhelmed when Sam Burns told me that a testimonial show was being put on for me, and it made me realise for the umpteenth time that I owe this guy more than I can ever tell.

To think that Sam wasn't exactly sold on the idea of being my manager when the idea was first put to him! I can just imagine how his old bonce tipped to one side in characteristic fashion as he said (reportedly) 'From what I hear, that man's rarely without a glass of Guinness in his hand. I'll bet he's a no-good bastard.' But we formed a bond of friendship and trust that will last. I'm proud of that, and I'm satisfied that I never once let him down. In his job as managing director of the William Hill Organization, this is something that he would probably have laid long odds against when we first teamed up!

But never once did I have any reason to query any fight or financial arrangement that he made for me. Naturally we 'discussed' things together, and there were probably times when he felt like telling me to piss off and not give him any more aggro, but softly-spoken Sam always kept his cool and his patience at those times when I probably fully deserved the elbow.

People often ask me whether I would like to have a son and see him grow into a champion. I've never really given up hoping that a son would be born to us, but the Duchess might have other ideas. I wouldn't mind a son of mine becoming a professional boxer, provided that there was someone around cast in the Sam Burns mould to guide him through a tough and very often perilous career.

I think I know a bit about the boxing game after all these years, but before I considered carrying on in some sort of capacity in boxing, I would want to be blessed with the knowledge, experience, and soft persuasion of Sam, combined with the driving force and no-mercy attitude of Freddie Hill. I've often cursed that sadistic bastard for the way he pushed me through the pain barrier in training, but what a bloke to have behind you in the corner!

Freddie, Sam, and I have been a trinity that is a rarity in my business, and I'm terribly sad that the relationship is no longer what it was, although I still see them both, of course, and get on extremely well with them. Without that pair I would never have got anywhere in the professional game. Although I was an Olympic gold medallist when we met, and obviously had some potential, I'm the sort of bloke who could easily have gone off the rails, especially in those early days, when all the money was such a novelty to me. I just hope that they feel that everything was worthwhile, and that I played my full part.

I was so bloody hypnotised by money in the early days that I even once considered buying Coppins, former home of the Duke and Duchess of Kent, which is less than half a mile from our front door in Iver. I could just see myself as the country squire, and when Cheryl used to kick me out of bed at some ungodly hour in the morning to start roadwork, I would often cock an eye at Coppins as I ran past, and the time came when this dream almost became a reality.

The Duke of Kent had been killed while flying in the last war, and when the Duchess died, Coppins came onto the market. With my ring earnings then in the ascendancy, I became interested, and such grand ideas naturally soon found their way into the newspapers. There were probably quite a few shudders at the prospect of the Finnegans moving in, but I kept the thing on the boil, for this sort of publicity doesn't do you any harm in the fight business. When it came to the crunch, of course, my funds didn't quite extend far enough, which was a pity, because Coppins was a place that I could have taken quite a pride in. There were those who recalled that I nearly got evicted from my old council house for not keeping the garden tidy, but those memories didn't bother me – I would have shown them a thing or two!

Coppins eventually went for about £250,000, but if I'd known that property prices were going to soar even higher, I might have tapped Sam or his tycoon mate Jarvis Astaire for a bit of help. Coppins is probably worth twice that much today.

But the days of dreaming are over, and one of my main preoccupations as I come towards the end of my own story is with younger brother Kevin. Sam and Freddie are helping him to regain his British and European middleweight supremacy, and

153

with me out of the way, and Kevin's shrewd brain, I'm sure he'll keep the family name up near the top for a while yet. I happen to know that he wasn't in a great frame of mind when he lost his British title to Alan Minter, and that's something which has irked him ever since, making him all the more determined to put the record straight all round.

I shall feel for him as Freddie drives him to the limit in that torture chamber at the Craven Arms, but it's a punishment that's got to be handed out. There is no place for any but the most dedicated in boxing, and this is something you have to learn if you're reaching for the top. Of course, you always go through times when you wonder if it's all worthwhile. I certainly did, but Cheryl was always there to keep me straight. If she'd been a feller, she would have been one of the most colourful and hardest-hitting fighters in the history of the sport. I know – I've tasted a few shots!

Now that we're moving into a new sphere in our lives, getting used to being out of boxing, and trying to organise ourselves for the future, it could be that we won't be seen at the ringside as much as we used to. This won't be because we're tired of boxing. It always gives me a kick to be introduced on fight night, and to climb up to the ring in a sharp suit with my red lot (gold watch and chain) spread across my waist. But there will be a great many other things to do.

British boxing doesn't want the likes of me hanging around bathing in the fading light of old glories. It needs new blood, new personalities in order to keep those turnstiles clicking. They're there somewhere, lurking around in some poxy job waiting for the big break, and I'll be watching closely to see who comes along. I

154

know what will be going on in their minds as they slog for the top, and my message to them is simple – give it all you've got, but still have fun.

For the record

Chris Finnegan as a professional

1968

Dec. 9 Mick Fleetham w. rsf. 3 Anglo-American SC.

Dec. 17 Dick Griffiths w. rsf. 4 Shoreditch.

1969

Jan. 14 Dervan Airey w. pts. 6 Bethnal Green.

Feb. 11 Liam Dolan w. pts. 6 Anglo-American SC.

Mar. 25 Larry Brown w. rtd. 5 Wembley.

May 6 Danny Ashie L. rsf. 2 (cut eye) Shoreditch.

Aug. 4 Brendan Ingle w. rsf. 8 (cut eye) Manchester Anglo.

Oct. 20 Ronnie Hough w. pts. 8 Anglo-American SC.

Dec. 8 Harry Scott w. pts. 10 Anglo-American SC.

1970

Jan 19 Francisco Ferri w. rsf. 6 Anglo-American SC.

Feb. 16 Ray Brittle w. rsf. 9 Anglo-American SC. (Southern Area light-heavyweight title)

Mar. 24 Hans Dieter Schwartz w rsf 6 Wembley.

Apr 21 Dervan Airey w. rsf. 4 Albert Hall.

May 21 Clarence Cassius w. rsf. 5 Anglo-American SC.

Aug 27 Tom Bogs L. pts. 15 Copenhagen. (European middle-weight title).

Oct 6 Guerrino Scattolin w. pts. 8 Albert Hall

1971

Jan. 24 Eddie Avoth w. rsf. 15 WSC. (British and Commonwealth light-heavyweight titles).

Mar. 29 Pete Riccitelli w. rsf. 4 Manchester Anglo.

156

May 5 Conny Velensek drew 15 Berlin. (European light-heavyweight title)
Sept. 9 Bob Benoit w. rsf. 8 Anglo-American SC.
Oct. 5 Roger Rouse w. rsf. 4 Albert Hall.
Oct. 19 Hal Carroll w. pts. 10 Albert Hall

1972
Feb. 1 Conny Velensek w. pts. 15 Nottingham. (European light-heavyweight title).
Mar 7 Jerry Evans w. rsf. 4 Albert Hall.
Apr. 18 Ronnie Wilson w. pts. 10 Nottingham.
June 6 Jan Lubbers w. ko. 8 Albert Hall. (European light-heavyweight title).
Sept. 26 Bob Foster L. ko. 14 Wembley. (world light-heavyweight title).
Nov. 14 Rudiger Schmidtke L. rsf. 12 (cut nose). Wembley. (European light-heavyweight title).

1973
Mar. 13 Roy John w. pts. 15 Wembley. (British and Commonwealth light-heavyweight titles).
Apr. 9 Brian Kelly Burden w. rsf. 4 Anglo-American SC.
May 22 John Conteh L. pts. 15 Wembley. (European, British and Commonwealth light-heavyweight titles).
Nov. 13 Mike Quarry w. pts. 10 Wembley.

1974
May 21 John Conteh L. rsf. 6 (cut scalp) Wembley. (European

British and Commonwealth light-heavyweight titles).
Oct. 1 Harold Richardson w. pts. 10 Wembley.
Dec. 2 Victor Attivor w. pts. 8 Anglo-American SC.

1975
June 3 Johnny Frankham L. pts. 15 Albert Hall (vacant British
light-heavyweight title).
Oct. 14 Johnny Frankham w. pts. 15 Albert Hall (British light-
heavyweight title).

CAREER BREAKDOWN: Total bouts – 36. Won 12 on points,
won 15 on interventions, won one by clean knockout. Lost three
on points, lost three because of injury, lost one on a clean knockout. Drew one.
